JOHN CUNNINGHAM

JOHN CUNNINGHAM

Second World War Night Fighter Ace and Test Pilot

PHILIP BIRTLES

FONTHILL

Fonthill Media Language Policy

Fonthill Media publishes in the international English language market. One language edition is published worldwide. As there are minor differences in spelling and presentation, especially with regard to American English and British English, a policy is necessary to define which form of English to use. The Fonthill Policy is to use the form of English native to the author. Philip Birtles was born and educated in Croydon; therefore, British English has been adopted in this publication.

Fonthill Media Limited
Fonthill Media LLC
www.fonthillmedia.com
office@fonthillmedia.com

First published in the United Kingdom and the United States of America 2023

British Library Cataloguing in Publication Data:
A catalogue record for this book is available from the British Library

Copyright © Philip Birtles 2023

ISBN 978-1-78155-871-3

Typeset in 11.5pt on13pt Sabon
Printed and bound in England

Contents

Foreword   7
Acknowledgements   9

1   Early Years   11
2   Combat in the Second World War   20
3   Rest Tour and Mosquito Operations   43
4   Return to de Havilland   65
5   Comets   81
6   Comet 4   102
7   Trident   112
8   Testing Moments   135

Appendix I: Deep-Stall Postscript   155
Appendix II: Sir Geoffrey's Chief Test Pilot   156
Appendix III: German Aircraft Destroyed/Probably
Destroyed/Damaged by John Cunningham (1940–1944)   159

Foreword

Group Captain John Cunningham was one of Britain's greatest flyers, legendary as a night fighter pilot and internationally famous as a test pilot. I had the privilege to get to know him late in his life. As a former fighter pilot myself, the radar skills I learnt in the 1960s were forged by John Cunningham.

It is difficult today to truly imagine the beginnings of air interception by night using airborne radar. The crudeness and unreliability of the early radar sets, operating in a constantly vibrating and cold environment, made mastering the technical, communication, and flying skills extraordinarily difficult. John Cunningham—together with his navigator, Jimmy Rawnsley—gained outstanding success by night, with twenty confirmed enemy aircraft destroyed beside three 'probable' and seven 'damaged'. The awarding of three DSOs and two DFCs to John Cunningham alone are testament to John and Jimmy's remarkable achievement.

Cunningham's later work as a test pilot is just as legendary. He was among the first to explore the boundaries of supersonic flight at a time when flying at such speed was little understood and often dangerous. He also took the world's first commercial jet airliner, the Comet, into the air on its maiden flight and thus ushered in a new era that was to have a transformational effect on travel across the world.

John Cunningham kept immaculate records of his night-fighting experiences and his test flying; both demonstrate his analytical skills, his tenacity and attention to detail. He was internationally respected as a test pilot and did much to promote British aviation both at home and abroad. His flying logbooks, together with the reports and notes he wrote of his experiences, and the author's many years of working with John Cunningham, form the basis of this book.

His life's work and contribution to British aviation, both in the air and as an ambassador, will never be surpassed. Many felt he deserved the recognition of a knighthood for his achievements, but he was perhaps too modest and self-effacing for this, and he never sought the limelight that he frequently faced. This book is a tribute to a most exceptional pilot and his inspirational leadership.

Air Marshal Sir Ian Macfadyen KCVO CB OBE
February 2020

Acknowledgements

It would not have been possible to write this biography without the kind agreement and support of Ms Melissa John, who is the owner of Group Captain Cunningham's medals and memorabilia, and to Gregory Muddell, who arranged for John's documents to be made available to us. We, and the foundation, are grateful to them both.

1

Early Years

In times of international tension and wars, demands for supremacy result in vast sums of money being invested in technology, not only in defence of freedom but also offensive operations. Over two world wars and many global campaigns since the end of the Second World War in 1945, rapid progress in aviation and weapons development has been made. In 1914, aeroplanes were fragile contraptions with unreliable engines, but by 1918, aviation had evolved with effective fighters for defence and bombers to take the offensive to the enemy.

During the interwar period, military aviation stagnated while civil aviation continued to progress with greater reliability and safety, providing passengers with the comfort of enclosed cabins. The RAF was equipped with biplane-era fighters and bombers that had advanced very little from the types available in 1918. The major developments were the monoplane Hurricane and Spitfire day fighters. Despite being a monoplane, the Hurricane still used Hawker biplane construction with fabric covering, but it was a rugged structure able to absorb battle damage and bring its pilot home safely. The Spitfire was an all-metal semi-monocoque structure that was more capable of development, with improvements continuing throughout the Second World War, but it was more demanding to build.

Not just airframes and engines improved, but also the systems and equipment, which was to benefit commercial aviation worldwide from 1945. Probably the greatest step forward was the development of the gas turbine engine, allowing speeds to be achieved well in excess of those capable by propeller-driven aircraft. Many of the scientists, often known as boffins, were unknown due to the classified nature of their work including the development of radar, although a number received recognition after the war, examples being Frank Whittle and Barnes Wallis.

However, the pilots gained media recognition due to their courageous exploits both in the Battle of Britain and for leading major raids into enemy territory. Although he was not strictly in the Battle of Britain, John Cunningham was destroying enemy raiders at night from the time of the Battle of Britain right through to the end of the war.

John was born in July 1917 to Arthur and Evelyn Cunningham, with two older sisters and a younger brother. His father was a senior executive in the Dunlop Rubber Company, and his mother was a full-time housewife. The family lived in a large comfortable house in Croydon, with John attending Bowden preparatory school in Newhaven as a boarder, until moving back to Croydon for his secondary education in Whitgift School. John had already gained a passion for aviation, his first flight being during summer 1926 in a venerable ex-RAF trainer Avro 504. When at Whitgift, he started a model aeroplane club and was a member of the school Army Officer Training Corps, giving him some experience of what service life may be like. Living in Croydon meant that he could easily cycle to the airport, which was still active then as London airport, stimulating his interest.

With his formal academic education coming to an end at Whitgift, John began to make preparations for his career, which was without doubt going to be in aviation. While a career in the RAF would satisfy his keenness to fly, he was interested in a greater depth of the challenges presented by aviation, the choice of companies being wide at that stage with Vickers at Weighbridge and Hawker at Kingston being the closest. There was also rearmament as a result of the threat of conflict from Germany, which spurred the advances in aircraft, systems, and armament development.

There was the possibility of attending university where he could have learned to fly with the university air squadron, but he elected for a more practical approach and in 1935 was successful in his application for an apprenticeship with the de Havilland Aeronautical School, which was second to none in aerospace training. The company had by that time located in a new factory on farmland at Hatfield. Geoffrey de Havilland was one of Britain's aviation pioneers, having made the first flight of an aircraft designed and built by him and his colleague Frank Hearle on 10 September 1910. Following his successful flight trials, it was the first aeroplane to be bought by the British government at the Royal Aircraft Factory at Farnborough, with Geoffrey being hired as designer and test pilot and Frank employed in engineering.

Geoffrey de Havilland went on to form the de Havilland Aircraft Company in September 1920 after working as designer and test pilot with Airco during the First World War. The de Havilland Company was always a family concern, as not only did the founder head up the organisation, but he continued to take a direct interest in the company developments, and also participated in test flying right up to the start of the Second World War. All three of his sons were active in the company, two as test pilots (both of whom lost their lives in the advancement of aviation) and Peter de Havilland, who was a salesman and demonstration pilot. The family atmosphere, which John felt very much part of, was also for the employees. If the breadwinner was employed by the company, there were often opportunities for wives to join in administration roles, and as their children grew up, they would often apply to join the company. Another benefit made by the company was to employ Dr Barnadoe's orphans, many staying with the company for many years.

John began his flying career during his early days in the de Havilland Aeronautical School. He joined 604 (County of Middlesex) Squadron in the Auxiliary Air Force (AAF) at Hendon, where he learned to fly. The Auxiliary squadrons were operated by a small core of permanent RAF personnel, manned by volunteer 'weekend' flyers who were trained to the same standard as regular aircrew, who, and in times of conflict, would join the regular RAF as part of the order of battle. Later, the RAF Volunteer Reserve was formed to provide a pool of trained aircrew to join existing, established squadrons. John's squadron had originally been formed as a bomber unit, but when joined, it was in the process of becoming a Hawker Demon-equipped fighter squadron. These biplanes were rapidly becoming obsolete with little advance from early 1920s technology, while Germany was known to be re-equipping with modern monoplane aircraft, which had allowed Luftwaffe aircrew to gain combat experience in the Spanish Civil War.

Many strategists believed in the concept of 'the bomber would always get through' with the belief that in any major war, air power and bombing would result in the destruction of major population and industrial areas, bringing surrender from an enemy. This was soon found to be untrue with early bombing operations being largely ineffectual.

After his initial training of some thirteen flying hours of instruction, John made his first solo in Avro Tutor J8451 on Sunday, 15 March 1936 for twenty-five minutes, followed by developing his skills, making his first solo in a combat type—Hawker Hart K5037—after three months of weekend flying basic training. By this time, he had a total flying time of fifty-four hours and twenty minutes, including dual and passenger times. Although he was not yet cleared to fly on combat training, he was certainly making progress towards being operational. In August 1936, John made his first solo in Hawker Demon as 604 Squadron made the transition from day bombers to a two-seat fighter unit.

With the coronation of King George VI, John flew one of four 604 Squadron Demons on a long-distance tour to visit other

AAF squadrons in the north of Britain as a useful cross-country navigation exercise. On Friday, 26 March 1937, the flight was made from Hendon to Leuchars near St Andrews in Scotland. On the way, they made a stop with 608 (North Riding) Squadron at Thornaby and then a short flight to 607 (County of Durham) at Usworth, before flying on to Leuchars, in a total flying time of three and a half hours. After a break of a day at Leuchars, the group flew on to Abbotsinch, now Glasgow Airport, where 602 (City of Glasgow) Squadron were based. The return was via Turnhouse, now Edinburgh airport, where 603 (City of Edinburgh) was based, and stopped overnight at Usworth before returning to Hendon on Monday 29 March.

During April, John continued his training with exercises to practice more for the combat roles, rather than just flying. These exercises included camera gun operation, battle climbs, and more navigation exercises. On 26 April, John made a night landing in an Avro Tutor, the first of many, and by the end of September, he had flown more than 259 hours and gained the proficiency assessment of above average.

Meanwhile, during the working week, John completed his three-year apprenticeship, where among the tasks were design and construction of the DH.94 Moth Minor, with his friend Phil Smith, who was later to become chief designer and director of de Havilland. They were part of the team working on this project sponsored by Captain de Havilland for a low-cost private owner aircraft, with two seats and a low monoplane wing, powered by a specially developed 90-hp Gipsy Minor engine.

In September 1937, Captain de Havilland's eldest son, Geoffrey, was appointed chief test pilot, when Bob Waite was killed flying the Tech School-designed TK 4 Racer. The only other members of the test pilot team were George Gibbins and Guy Tucker, who had an enormous workload consisting of production Tiger Moths, Queen Bees, Rapides, and Oxfords. In addition, the new Albatross four-engined airliner was nearly ready for flight testing, followed by the lacklustre Don multi-role trainer and the all-metal Flamingo. The captain was well aware of John's growing flying experience with the RAF and suggested that he might like to join the team to assist with test flying the Moth Minors. By this time, he had realised his ambition was to be less involved in design but in the manufacture of aircraft, or better still, in flight testing, becoming the fourth member of the team on 20 April 1938.

Captain de Havilland had made the maiden flight of the Moth Minor, and John was allocated to test flying production Moth Minors, with an interest showed by the captain. With flying duties in demand and availability of many aeroplane needing testing, there were no formal working hours, and as there were no fixed lunch facilities, John would meet up with Geoffrey Jnr for a pint of beer and a bowl of soup at the Crooked Chimney near Lemsford, a long-term favourite for John and the other test pilots into the jet age.

In June 1938, John was testing a Hornet Moth with a nosewheel undercarriage, and by early 1939, he had almost completed flight testing of the first production Moth Minor. He thought it would be prudent for Geoffrey Jnr to fly it for his opinion on any variations with the hand-built prototype. Geoffrey was very busy with testing the Flamingo, but John insisted, as he was only a junior pilot, and needed the opinion of an experienced test pilot. Geoffrey agreed and suggested that he would do aft centre of gravity spinning tests, with John in the other cockpit to provide a representative load. The two pilots climbed into the Moth Minor on 11 April 1939, with no anti-spin parachute fitted as recovery had been so docile with the prototypes.

They took off with John in the rear cockpit and climbed to 8,000 feet, when Geoffrey initiated a left-hand spin, making a recovery after eight turns. Climbing back up to 8,000 feet, Geoffrey selected a right-hand spin, but during the first revolution, the engine stopped and the nose reared up, the aircraft entering a flat spin, resulting in loss of control. After a few turns, Geoffrey asked John to have a try at regaining control, but John had no success and suggested to Geoffrey that they abandon the aircraft, to which he agreed. They both stepped out of the aircraft on to the wing, and as they pulled their rip cords and started descending, the Moth Minor dropped its nose and recovered from the spin on its own. The propeller began windmilling, which restarted the engine, with the ignition still switched on, the aircraft circling the descending pilots, with a danger of it hitting them. Fortunately, the aircraft descended rapidly and crashed into a large oak tree near Wheathamsted before bursting into flames. On landing rather heavily, John took out his camera and photographed the wreckage and his parachute spread out on the ground. John hitched a lift in a passing car, which took him to the Crooked Chimney, where he knew Geoffrey would be found. After a few beers with colleagues who had gathered, Geoffrey said something along the lines of 'Now we've got a job to do. You'd better get on with it. That'll keep you busy'.

John was kept busy spinning the Moth Minor to make sure it was safe to fly, resulting in an increase in rudder travel and additional rudder area below the tailplane. Also anti-spin strakes were fitted on the upper fuselage forward of the fin, as had also been done with Tiger Moths. As a result, John's efforts were rewarded with seventy-one built before production had to be stopped due to space being required for urgent production in the Second World War.

John continued flying with 604 Squadron, taking off from Hendon on 10 October in a Demon to make the short flight to North Weald, but had to return to Hendon due to engine problems. The significance of this otherwise routine flight was that for the first time he had AC Jimmy Rawnsley as his gunner; the pair of them went on to make a highly effective night-fighting team during the war years. In April 1938, John flew another long-distance navigation flight from Hendon to Castletown near Wick in the north of Scotland, returning three days later along the east coast with stops at Montrose, Turnhouse, and Usworth.

In addition to daytime flying, John was also building up his night-flying experience, while the country was making preparations for conflict. On 5 May, he spent one hour and forty minutes on co-operation exercises with searchlight batteries on the ground, giving the crews experience in finding aircraft. Once war started, night fighters worked with searchlights and anti-aircraft guns to help defend against the raiders until the development of Airborne Interception (AI) radar. Two nights later, John was airborne again, assessing the effectiveness of the blackout in Slough.

To maintain public interest in the RAF, each year, there were Empire Air Days held at a number of regional airfields, with aircraft lined up on static display, flypasts of current service aircraft, mock battles demonstrating air strength, and aerobatics. John was involved in a number of these events, requiring planning and preparation. Later in May 1938, he was practicing dive-bombing and display flying for the Hendon Pageant.

By the start of August 1938, John had flown 348 hours and thirty minutes with the RAF and continued to receive an above average assessment again from his commanding officer. In addition, his civil flying with de Havilland had reached 239 hours and thirty-five minutes.

At the start of 1939, 604 Squadron began to re-equip with twin-engined Bristol Blenheim monoplanes. It was an all-metal aircraft designed as a light bomber and was totally unsuitable as a fighter. It was armed with powered gun turret on top of the fuselage behind the wing trailing edges, and there was provision for a ventral gun pack with four Browning .303-inch machine guns, gaining the designation Mk If. With the requirement for night fighters becoming apparent, and no aircraft specifically designed for the role, the Blenheim was considered as a suitable interim answer. John flew his first solo in a Blenheim on 19 February 1939, and he was not impressed. It was useless with poor visibility, lacked radar, and it was no faster than the bombers it was meant to catch and destroy.

By July 1939, John was mainly flying Blenheims, but on 10 July, he had the opportunity of flying a Hurricane for the first time, which was a great improvement on the earlier Hawker biplanes and a modern fighter for the time. With war almost inevitable in August 1939, the Auxiliary Air Force merged into the RAF order of battle. On 23 August 1939, John received his 'Notice of Calling Out', requiring him to report at Hendon Aerodrome by 10 a.m. the following day, putting 604 Squadron and the other Auxiliaries on a war footing.

With his call up in the war to fly with the RAF, he was well prepared to return to de Havilland after the war, returning to a more demanding test flying role. John was instrumental in the development of Airborne Interception (AI) radar during the war and went on to lead the development of the Comet, the world's first commercial jet airliner, followed by the Trident, the first jet airliner to land automatically in all weathers. His legacy to aviation is enormous and lasting, with his total commitment to flying. He was very professional in everything he did, and built a team around him with similar high skills and approach to life. He was a perfectionist, maintaining high standards, and did not suffer fools gladly. John was a modest gentleman who did not seek publicity, but would promote the company and aircraft enthusiastically at whatever level. In addition to maintaining his flying logbooks, which were used regularly for reference to a particular incident, he also kept detailed notebooks covering his activities and travels, allowing his experiences to be taken into account when in discussions with members of the design team. John would often walk around the shop floor of the flight test hangar, talking to the fitters and supervision, whose names he knew well.

2

Combat in
the Second World War

The day war was declared, the squadrons were in readiness for enemy bombing attacks against British cities, although they did not happen. John made his first operational sortie on 6 September, but it was a false alarm, returning to base; it was not until 19 September that he flew his first night raid.

Meanwhile, John and the rest of 604 Squadron had been dispersed from Hendon to tented accommodation at North Weald, where regular squadrons were in permanent accommodation in the main camp. Although initially the autumn weather was not too bad, it later turned very cold with no heating in the Blenheims or the crew flying suits. Their main duties were long-range shipping patrols along the North Sea coast as far north as the Humber Estuary, in bitterly cold discomfort with insufficient protection against the extreme temperatures. As the aircraft climbed, the temperature in the cockpit dropped rapidly, the air being searing cold to breath, causing the eyes to stream, and ice could even form inside the face mask. As a result, considerable concentration was required to make sensible decisions. In addition to being uncomfortable with the cold, the North Sea patrols were incredibly boring and non-productive. During one patrol of four hours, John became so stiff that to exercise his frozen muscles, he moved across to the navigator's seat, while keeping his hands on the control wheel. To ensure the best levels of instrument serviceability, daily night-flying tests (NFT) were carried out.

With few pilots having any night-flying experience, night patrols could be hazardous, particularly in all weathers and combat conditions. The Demons had been fairly benign machines, but flying the more advanced twin-engined Blenheims at night with the mandatory blackout, provided no landmarks, and with winter weather flying, was blind. There were no homing beacons and no possibility of being talked down on the final approach and landing at the airfield. Blind flying instruments were not totally reliable, with poor radio communications that were weak and only available at short range.

It was hardly surprising that a number of the 604 Squadron pilots were killed, with many accidents being caused by stalling after take-off or pilots becoming disorientated when turning at low altitude and hitting the ground; the rate of losses unrelated to actual combat was alarmingly high. Despite risks, the squadron was gaining experience of operating at night in all weathers. However, lack of training, lack of overall experience, and unfamiliarity with new untried equipment added to the accident rate. The worst enemy at the time was known as 'the dreaded Isaac' after Isaac Newton's laws of gravity, but John's flying skills credited him with being as near to 'Isaac proof' as possible (because John's flying skills appeared to almost defy gravity), according to Jimmy Rawnsley.

In 8 January 1940, while on escort duties with the Thames/Humber convoys, John was asked to fly a circuit on long-nosed Blenheim P4847, with some secret equipment on board, intended to assist with the interception of another aircraft at night. John flew with Sergeant Horder and an air gunner on an hour's sortie carrying what was in fact the first time a purpose-designed AI radar was installed in an aircraft.

In mid-January, the squadron moved to RAF Northolt, which was covered in snow when they arrived, with rumours of a posting to warmer climates, in contrast to the conditions they had come from. However, it was an elaborate security hoax as the Blenheims carried civil registrations and were marked with the blue swastika of Finland, the pilots tasked to deliver the aircraft to Finland via Sweden, to provide Finland with aircraft to fight their Russian aggressors. The Blenheims were difficult enough to engine start in the cold British climate, let alone Arctic conditions in Finland, even though they had been supplied with a special warming device. Before the 604 Squadron crews could depart to help with the introduction of the Blenheims, there was a Soviet victory over the Finns, resulting in a peace and neutrality agreement in mid-March 1940. Fifteen months later, Hitler invaded the Soviet Union, who then became our Allies.

During February, March, and April, in addition to NFTs, John's activities included sector reconnaissance, minelaying patrol escort, formation flying at night, co-operation with searchlights, and firing guns on the ranges at Sutton Bridge in the Wash. On 22 April, three 604 Squadron Blenheims were tasked with escorting Winston Churchill, then first lord of the Admiralty, in a de Havilland Flamingo to Le Bourget for a meeting of the Supreme War Council in Paris to discuss the serious situation in Norway, which had been occupied by the Germans.

While taxying at Northolt, John had his tailwheel tyre burst, but it was quickly repaired. John's gunner was Jimmy, as a leading aircraftman, and the air attaché provided accommodation in an excellent Paris hotel, where they heard anti-aircraft fire for the first time. Churchill attended a second meeting the next morning to discuss the possibility of Germany attacking Holland and Belgium, with the Blenheims escorting the return flight later in the day. As anticipated, German forces invaded Holland, Belgium, and Luxembourg on 10 May, resulting in a British National Government being formed the following day, with Churchill as prime minister and minister of defence. From this point, Churchill was able to be in charge of the Allied defence policy, ending the Phoney War and bringing action on all fronts.

One of Churchill's confidants and advisors was Professor Lindeman, who came up with a rather impractical idea of defending against major attack by Luftwaffe bombers. The plan was to drop bombs fitted with photo-electric cells into a bomber stream, and when a target was detected, it would explode. No. 604 Squadron was designated to undertake the trials with John nominated, as probably the most experienced pilot available. John was not impressed with the plan and was briefed at Bentley Priory, the HQ of Fighter Command, following which he was sent to Exeter for the trials working with a team from the Royal Aircraft Establishment (RAE). Trials commenced with dropping smoke-filled bombs against balloons, later followed by the more realistic target towed by a Hawker Henley. When a bomb exploded prematurely as it left the Blenheim, filling the aircraft with smoke, John was relieved to learn further trials had been cancelled. This incident became known in Fighter Command as 'John's bomb'.

On 15 May 1940, 604 Squadron moved from Northolt to the forward airfield at Manston to carry operations over the Channel, with the German war machine advancing rapidly across the Low Countries. All RAF airfields in France had been abandoned, and with the approach of the desperate evacuation of the remnants of the British Expeditionary Force (BEF) from Dunkirk, there was total chaos with burning ships and enemy guns shelling the thousands of retreating troops on the crowded beaches. Following the small ships evacuating many of our surviving troops, but with their arms and equipment abandoned on the beach, there was a lull in the German advances as they consolidated in preparation for the next move. There were new personnel additions to the squadron to replace casualties, promotions, and postings, with 604 moving to Middle Wallop on 26 July 1940, briefly staying at Gravesend. On arrival at their new station, the unit was designated a full-time night fighter squadron.

Work commenced on fitting mysterious 'black boxes' into Blenheims by a mass of technicians and boffins, with a new breed of aircraftmen who had no knowledge of aircraft, but who were to operate the new equipment, which was officially designated as Airborne Interception (AI) or radio location, later called radar. Despite the secrecy, there was no doubt Fighter Command was determined to develop night fighting, and 604 Squadron was very much involved with the service introduction of combat operations.

Not long after the squadron arrived, the airfield was bombed, causing serious damage, particularly to hangars and the technical site. The grass airfield was still being prepared, and dispersal accommodation was very primitive, with the crews on standby in full flying gear as there was still no heating in the aircraft, and temperatures at operational altitudes could be as low as -30 degrees C. As night fighters, the Blenheims were too slow to catch enemy bombers, with the result that no claims were made.

During this time, the airfield was busy with Hurricanes and Spitfires fighting in the Battle of Britain, and the Blenheims were training during the day with flying operations at night. In an attempt to improve the speed differential, the gun turret was removed, resulting in the gunners being posted out or volunteering to train as radar operators. This was the chance Jimmy took with enthusiasm as he could be in at the start of a new technology programme, which must develop in the future.

In the late summer of 1940, despite fitting of the new AI radar, without overall guidance, it was impossible for the crews to locate enemy night bombers close enough for the pilot to see it, identify it as hostile, and attack. Attempting to night fight in extremely primitive conditions was hazardous, with no external references and using less than reliable instruments. John pointed out that the country was at war, and night fighting was a very special skill, requiring a great determination despite the challenging conditions. The difficulties had to be overcome, with John being determined to set high standards for others to follow.

The normal duty roster at Middle Wallop was for two nights on call, followed by two nights off, although when not flying at night, there were the regular daily flying duties. When on night-flying duties, there would be a meal in the mess beforehand, and after the operations, there would be the customary bacon and eggs, which were a luxury due to food rationing. Amid rumours of new aircraft equipment in September, John was promoted to squadron leader in charge of 'B' Flight, with Jimmy becoming the senior gunner on the flight. Just before the end of the month, the new formidable and pugnacious Bristol Beaufighter was delivered, with the first pilot to convert being the CO, Mike Anderson, followed by John.

Like most new aircraft, the Beaufighter suffered from teething troubles due to insufficient development flying in combat conditions prior to issue to squadrons. One of the fundamental problems was with the illuminated gun sight, the brightness of which was uncontrollable, it being either full brilliance, or not on at all. John reported the problem to the Night Fighting Committee at Bentley Priory, led by Air Marshal Sir Sholto Douglas through Professor Tizard, which was referred to the RAE at Farnborough. Among the boffins was A. A. Hall, who was a gunsight expert; he redesigned the rheostat operation to allow full variation in brightness, without the pilot losing his night vision. John was therefore working with the man who later became Sir Arnold Hall, chairman and managing director of Hawker Siddeley Group, which took over de Havilland in 1960.

During this period, development work had been continuing on a radar control system on the ground at Middle Wallop, and John was an adviser on what was to become ground control interception (GCI), which as it improved was able to direct the night fighter crew close enough to the target for it to be located by the onboard AI radar, followed by visual recognition, the Beaufighter being fast enough to catch the raider. The system used was AI Mk IV with an arrowhead antenna transmitter in the nose and receiver aerials on the wing tips.

The station commander, Grp Capt. 'Bill' Elliot, served in the First World War and took a special interest in 604 Squadron, using his influential contacts to his advantage. Whenever there was a significant problem, he would arrange contact with the most appropriate person or organisation. When stability problems were

experienced with the new Beaufighters, John was able to contact
Sholto Douglas directly, who told John to fly to Bristol and have
them cure the problem. John was later to work with Sholto Douglas
when he was chairman of BEA and John's customer for Trident
airliners. When John flew to Filton, weights were attached to the
control column to tighten the elevator controls, and later, the
tailplane dihedral was increased improving longitudinal stability.

The Blitz commenced on 8 September 1940, as the Battle of
Britain gradually wound down. London was the initial target, with
the enemy bombers flying up the Thames estuary, which was easily
seen from the air at night. Full priority was given to the development
of tactics with the AI radar and GCI control, with Air Marshal Sir
Philip Jouber (assistance chief of the air staff (Radar), who regularly
called into Middle Wallop on his way to meet scientists, technicians,
and controllers) gaining first-hand information on the operational
requirements. John was also called to regular meetings with Sholto
Douglas at Bentley Priory.

During September and October 1940, John flew both Blenheims
and Beaufighters in what were known as 'Worth' patrols, flying
at night in a straight line east of Worth Matravers on the Dorset
coast, with Jimmy in the Blenheim gun turret. With the reduction in
activity from the Battle of Britain, John was able to take up trainee
operators from the AI school, in addition to stability checks, often
making sorties by day in the less hostile sky. Then in November, the
Luftwaffe changed their tactics and began to bomb the industrial
cities of the Midlands and the North, causing considerable damage
and having virtual immunity from interception.

On the night of 19–20 November, John was airborne in his
Beaufighter with John Phillipson as his radar operator with enemy
aircraft about, one of which was located by GCI that vectored John
into its direction. John saw a concentration of searchlights on the
clouds nearby and headed towards them, with Phillipson making a
good positive contact, gradually guiding John towards the target. In
the dark ahead, John detected some star-like lights, forming into a
dark shape that vanished when he looked directly at it.

Moving closer, the silhouette took shape and he called, 'I can see it'. By skilfully manoeuvring below the contact, he was able to identify it as a Ju 88—an enemy aircraft. John reduced power behind the bomber, maintaining his range behind the aircraft, and fired his 20-mm cannons. The Junkers fell and hit the ground with a massive explosion. This was the first time a Beaufighter had been successful in destroying an enemy bomber, justifying all the effort that had gone into developing the components of the night fighting systems. This interception had been preceded by two other successes, both by Fg Off. Ashfield of the Fighter Interception Unit (FIU) based at Ford flying a radar-equipped Blenheim, the first being in July 1940.

The news of the success was sent to Group HQ, Fighter Command, and the Air Ministry. To confirm it was no fluke, a few nights later, CO Mike Anderson destroyed a He 111. At this time, there were only three 604 Squadron crew operational on Beaufighters, with an urgent requirement for more Blenheim crews to be trained on the new aircraft, and by the end of 1940, six crews had qualified as operational on the new more effective type, allowing for Beaufighters to replace the slower Blenheims.

November 1940 was an exceptional time for John Cunningham, as in addition to his first success with an AI-equipped Beaufighter, he was called to a meeting with Sir Charles Portal, the chief of the air staff, to be told his former boss, Captain Geoffrey de Havilland, had asked Portal if he could borrow John for a day to fly the new Mosquito, which had been flown for the first time by Geoffrey Jnr on 25 November. The captain wished for an assessment of the new high-speed aircraft to check its suitability as a night fighter. On 2 February 1941, John flew his Beaufighter to Hatfield, when he was excited to get his first glimpse of the Mosquito, which had a marvellous shape and was a typically elegant DH aircraft. John became the first serving pilot to fly the new aircraft, following Geoffrey Jnr and George Gibbins. John found the aircraft light on the controls with the performance matching its elegance, convincing him that it had a great night fighter potential. Soon after the prototype was delivered to Boscombe Down for service trials, it was assessed by Allen Wheeler, who was not the first RAF pilot to fly the Mosquito.

Meanwhile, Jimmy Rawnsley had been training to become an AI operator, with the obvious aim of flying with John. While Jimmy was training and also continuing as a gunner on the remaining Blenheims, Phillipson was working with John, gaining air experience and operating the challenging AI. Jimmy's only way of obtaining practical experience was to fly in the Beaufighter as third crew member and persuade the regular operator to let him experience the operation. Jimmy was not able to join John's crew as it was important to achieve operational capability with the experienced operators first. Despite Jimmy being concerned he would not be ready when the Beaufighters became fully operational, he spent a lot of time in the special signals section, gaining experience and information. His turn came up in October.

His first sortie was with an instructor, and he was disappointed by the faintness of the barely recognisable blip that merged with the other interference on the screen. There was still a long way to go on the development of the AI radar to make it fully capable in combat. On Jimmy's second sortie, with John flying the training Blenheim and Bernard Cannon as instructor, Jimmy was unable to hold on to the blip and kept losing it. Sitting down in the mess afterwards, he began to work out where he might be going wrong and discovered he was directing the turn too far, stopping it sooner; also, holding a convergent course would prevent excessive course corrections.

After relaxing by watching a movie on his return to Middle Wallop, he joined a scratch crew as gunner, climbing through cloud and drizzle, but on reaching 17,000 feet, the aircraft experienced severe icing. The pilot descended to 5,000 feet, but lost control, and when he could not communicate with the pilot, Jimmy baled out; as he was landing, he saw the that control had been regained and the Blenheim was touching down. Jimmy learned that the pilot had ordered him to bale out, but as his intercom plug was not connected, the message had not got through. With Beaufighters becoming operational, Jimmy was keen to join John, and he was finally sent aloft in a turretless Blenheim with a sergeant pilot on a night patrol at 17,000 feet. He came close to his first big chance, but the enemy bomber was detected on the screen and was heading straight towards them, coming close to a collision, and losing contact.

The Luftwaffe were sending pathfinding Heinkels from Cherbourg to mark targets in the Midlands, equipped with a special blind bombing aid called X-Gerät, leading in the main enemy bomber force. The pathfinders therefore became the main targets. The aircraft took off just as it was getting dark, crossing the English coast between the Isle of Wight and Portland Bill; the defending night fighters aimed to catch the raiders while they were over the Channel.

John was in the forefront of this action, and on 23 December, he departed Middle Wallop with Phillipson. At 5 p.m., when it was nearly dark, they saw a Heinkel approaching from about 50 miles out to sea. At 15,000 feet, it was still light, and John stalked the target, firing his cannons, hitting the bomb load, which exploded violently; the aircraft went into a vertical dive through the cloud base below.

This added to his first success on 20 November, giving confidence that the RAF were able to combat the night bomber attacks, but the use of the secret AI radar could not be divulged to the public or even many in the services, creating a legend. The media were allowed to publish pictures of John Cunningham, who was credited with exceptional night vision, which permitted him see in the dark, like a cat, resulting in the title 'Cat's Eyes Cunningham'. It was said that he ate lots of carrots, which supposedly helped his night vision. John was very modest of his achievements, considering the 'Cat's Eyes' nickname a deception, but it did make the people of Great Britain understand that the RAF had a practical night fighter deterrent to German bombers, which had become vulnerable. Over a two-month period, 604 Squadron were able to destroy thirty hostile bombers, resulting in the Luftwaffe crews believing that either the techniques had improved or there was something special being used, although the Cunningham press stories had effectively maintained the secret of AI.

Improvements were made to scores in early 1941, including the interception of the enemy pathfinders over the Channel, but more important was the introduction of GCI stations along the south coast, allowing every night fighter to be directed by one controller. The controller followed the entire interception on a large cathode ray tube, bringing the RAF night fighters to within 1 mile or so behind the raider, allowing the AI operator to make contact. The GCI station that generally controlled 604 Squadron was at Sopley with the call sign 'Starlight'. It consisted of a revolving antenna surrounded by a few wooden huts, scattered vehicles, and a camouflaged caravan. The centre of the controller's desk was a large cathode ray tube with an outline of the local coast line marked on the face. All aircraft within range of this display, known as plan position indicator (PPI), appeared as small blips, which were shown in relationship to the map. Readings were supplied by airmen and airwomen, passing on to others at the end of the caravan, who in turn plotted the aircraft tracks using navigation computers, working out courses and speeds. Aircraft altitudes were established from operators at another cathode ray tube.

To maintain complete coverage of the area, the antenna turned in full circles, but if the controller needed to concentrate on a particular area of interest, by pressing a button, the antenna could be stopped, or reversed, to direct the beam in a particular direction. Power for turning the antenna was from two unfortunate airmen below, who pedalled a contraption somewhat like a tandem. When a target was detected and they were pedalling as hard as they could, they were unable to see any of the drama overhead, the two airmen being known as 'The Binders'.

Early in 1941, following sheer persistence and dedication, Jimmy was able to rejoin John, becoming his regular radar operator. His long previous partnership had created an understanding of John's method of operation, combining his patience and Jimmy's honesty, establishing a close working bond between them. When he did make mistakes, Jimmy owned up to them, learning by experience for the future. It was in mid-February that the team were together for the dusk trap of Pathfinder He 111s of KGr 100.

Their patrol commenced by heading out over Bournemouth in a clear glowing sky, Poole Harbour being recognisable below. Their patrol area was reached at 15,000 feet, around 40 miles south of Lulworth, flying along the designated route, with the AI turned on and warmed up ready for action, searching intently to the southwest from where the raiders approached. After a few minutes, the controller identified an approaching bomber flying at 15,000 feet and on track. John then began the cat and mouse game, dropping down to 11,500 feet into the misty dusk, leaving the enemy visual against the sky above.

John continued on his track, turning back at the end of the orbit, when Jimmy spotted the enemy aircraft, high above on the port quarter some way away, but clearly visible. John turned the Beaufighter sharply around, with the Heinkel approaching fast and high overhead. John stayed vertically below, watching through the roof panel as the unsuspecting raider flew on. John followed for ten minutes, waiting for darkness to approach, and when the Dorset coast was reached, the Heinkel began to orbit followed by John over Lyme Bay.

Just as night was descending, John attacked by increasing power climbing towards the target, which was growing larger as they approached. Jimmy checked the readiness of the 20-mm cannons, advising John that everything was ready with nothing behind. 'Good,' said John, 'Here goes'. The Heinkel sank into the line of fire when John fired the guns, with hits on the starboard engine followed by a further attempt at firing, but nothing happened. Jimmy rapidly reloaded the cannons, but by then, the Heinkel had vanished; although the controller still had contact, John descended to 3,000 feet but was still unable to make contact. Jimmy was concerned that he should have been monitoring the AI signal before reloading the guns, but then a few miles ahead, a stick of incendiaries fell to the ground, followed by the explosion of the Heinkel crashing to destruction.

With the increased losses of enemy bombers to RAF night fighters, the Luftwaffe crews began to constantly change course and height, with violent evasive action, and more alert gunners. Still in 1941, the Germans were lagging behind in AI radar development, although progress was being made. The Special Signals Unit at Middle Wallop had set up a homing beacon, enabling 604 Squadron crews to pick up the signal on their AI equipment from a range of 50 miles, guiding the pilots back without having to use the busy radio channels for bearings back to base. A new and improved airfield lighting system was installed, and if the weather deteriorated a new Standard Beam Approach (SBA) system had been installed to assist the approach and landing to avoid diversions.

In May 1941, John flew back to Hatfield with Jimmy for a check flight in the Mosquito NF Mk II prototype W4052, which Geoffrey de Havilland Jnr had flown out of a field adjacent to Salisbury Hall on 15 May to save a month of dismantling and reassembly. Geoffrey took John up initially and then let him fly it solo. John returned most enthusiastic with the possibilities of this aircraft fitted with AI radar, putting the RAF in the forefront of night fighting.

By the spring of 1941, the local GCI was working well, with more successes being made by 604 Squadron crews, creating a competitive spirit throughout the squadron. Crews were keen to be first off in the evenings to have the best chance of an interception, while senior officers were keen to learn more about the new system. John often had wing commanders and group captains who would become leaders of new night fighter squadrons. The original Auxiliary Air Force volunteers began to move on to more senior posts and were replaced by regular RAF officers. The new CO was Wg Cdr Charles Appleton, who had completed a tour in Bomber Command flying Whitleys. However, he had difficulty mastering the Beaufighter flying technique, as well as not understanding the jargon of the radar operators.

Then followed an unexpected arrival of Plt Off. Derek Jackson, who was a university professor, a highly qualified physicist, and an amateur jockey who had ridden in the Grand National. He wore the air gunners' badge, which was inappropriate, as he was very familiar with reading cathode ray tubes, operating them with ease, and the new CO adopted him as his operator. Not only was he a very skilled operator, but he could troubleshoot any problems experienced by the other crews.

Another significant member of 604 Squadron was 'Rory' Chisholm, who had been a member of the squadron in the 1930s, flying Wapitis before working in the Persian oilfields until returning to Britain when war broke out. Restarting his flying training, he was able to rejoin the squadron, bringing his engineering practical experience. He strove for excellence in everything he did, like John, but found flying the Beaufighter a challenge, in addition to struggling to understand and master the AI-controlled interception techniques, being both critical of himself and his easy-going radar operator Sergeant Bill Ripley. However, despite this difficult partnership, they complemented each other and were able to score some successes.

John was responsible for defining the operational techniques, making them seem simple and effortless, even though he worked very hard to achieve success. One example was if he ever made an unsatisfactory landing, day or night, he would take off immediately and try again. John set the standards for others to follow, allowing them to take on further responsibilities in leadership.

Throughout April 1941, heavy raids by the Luftwaffe continued. On 15 April, he and Jimmy managed to score a hat-trick. On the initial sortie that night, he shot down a He 111 over Monmouthshire with just forty rounds, and after returning to Middle Wallop, he was sent on a second sortie to reinforce the cab-rank standing patrols. While waiting for Starlight to identify an incoming target, John spotted searchlights to the north near Marlborough and was given permission to investigate. He turned around to what was believed to be a returning bomber, but the blip on the cathode ray tube would not stabilise. John responded by diving at increased power, allowing Jimmy to make contact, bringing the target within visual range. All of a sudden, the original blip became surrounded by interference, which they realised was the Southampton barrage balloons. John gained a visual sighting, identifying the target as a Heinkel; he fired, causing the enemy aircraft to flick over into a dive. John followed it down, but at 9,000 feet, he decided that the balloons were getting too close and eased out of the dive, although a large explosion from the ground indicated a positive success.

On heading back to base, they were soon back overhead Middle Wallop at 17,000 feet, giving him the height advantage on the fast-returning enemy bombers. Starlight identified a returning bomber, so they vectored John north-west, swinging him back onto the tail of the bandit. John was however 6,000 feet too high and descended gradually with Jimmy maintaining contact with the target until they found themselves approaching Southampton again. John then saw moonlight reflected off the Perspex of another He 111, closing to 80 yards; after a short salvo, the enemy aircraft burst into flames, impacting the Beaufighter with burning wreckage as John broke away high and to port, the third success crashing near Lymington.

A few weeks later, on 7 May, HRH King George VI was paying a visit, resulting in a great deal of tidying up on the station. All aircrew were to parade, and Charles Appleton CO of 604 Squadron ensured that his aircrew all wore the best blues, while the other two Middle Wallop squadrons paraded in their flying clothes. With dusk just approaching over Danesbury Hill, John was due to take the first patrol under the control of Starlight, with little time to spare before his take off. The king arrived, escorted by the AOC, Air Marshall Sir Sholto Douglas, and had a few words with the pilots. The king noticed some of the men on parade were not wearing flying badges and commented to Sholto Douglas, with a note being made.

On moving along the line, he came to Jimmy and asked him how many successes he had achieved, the reply being nine aircraft. The king requested that he get another one that night, especially for him. With the formalities completed, the king was driven to the Starlight base at Sopley, to be guided round by Sqn Ldr Brown, the chief controller. As the king departed Middle Wallop, there was a rush to the mess by 604 Squadron to get ready for action, and although a little delayed, the first Beaufighters took off for the patrol line over the Channel.

On arrival at his patrol altitude, John reported to Starlight, with the king present, a raider being detected approaching over the Channel towards Sopley. John was vectored by Brown on to heading 330, then 310 with Jimmy's eyes fixed on the cathode ray tube, which showed a clear image, but no contact. Brown gave John a final vector of 360, positioned 3 miles behind the target, and John increased power, the PPI display at GCI bringing the two blips together in the view of the king. Finally, the two blips appeared to merge into one, with Jimmy having locating the enemy bomber 2 miles ahead and well below them. While still over the sea at a range of around 4,000 feet, John saw the target, but the ambient light was still too bright, so in case he was spotted, John delayed his approach until they were over land where he would not be as visible.

The controller suggested to his audience that they went outside to maybe witness the interception, and as they were going down the steps, the approaching aircraft could be heard. John positioned 'R' for Robert behind and just below the Heinkel, pulling up until he was dead astern, getting the unsuspecting bandit in his sights, and fired. John pulled away to avoid damage from the wreckage as a small fire glowed in the aircraft; with the hydraulics hit, the undercarriage came down. Flying alongside, the Beaufighter watched the fire take hold, with the stricken aircraft going into a steep dive with flames streaming to the rear. The Beaufighter returned to Middle Wallop to have its twelfth victory painted on the tail fin.

John retired to bed, as he was due at a Fighter Command conference the next day, but when he returned, he was told his Beaufighter R2101 'R' had been destroyed. It was being flown by another crew later in the night, who had destroyed a Heinkel, but an engine had been hit by one of the raider's gunners, causing it to catch fire, and the crew had to abandon the aircraft. The replacement was T4625.

John had been awarded the DFC (Distinguished Flying Cross) in March, and following his 'hat trick' in April, a DSO (Distinguished Service Order) was added, while Jimmy was awarded a DFM (Distinguished Flying Medal). A few weeks later, Jimmy received a bar to his DFM, by which time he was a flight sergeant, and then commissioned. John's comments were that decorations and promotions were nice to have, but part of the continuing task ahead. Mastering the effective operation of the radar was a priority and left little time to consider career advancement or achieving decorations. Many had been killed, and John was thankful to have survived so far but did not feel he could plan too far ahead.

With the German launch of Operation Barbarossa (the invasion of Russia on 22 June), night bombing of Britain reduced significantly during May and June while the enemy preparations were made, the USSR as a result becoming an ally. Luftwaffe tactics changed to bombing raids approaching from over the Wash, heading for targets in the industrial cities of the Midlands. There were also roving enemy night fighters attacking the vulnerable returning RAF bombers, picking off the aircraft in the congestion around the east of England airfields.

John took 'B' Flight to Coltishall, to provide some defence while 255 Squadron became operational with their new Merlin-powered Beaufighter IIs. John had a close escape when the gunner from a Heinkel he was stalking set fire to one engine, causing the other to misfire while they were still well out over the sea. Fortunately, the engine picked up, returning safely to Coltishall. They jumped out rapidly as the engine was still burning, but apart from Jimmy injuring his head on a protruding bolt, they were unhurt.

The low-flying Ju 88 intruders were approaching at high speed below the coverage of the GCI stations. It was obvious to John that a faster aircraft such as the Mosquito and improved AI radar would be needed to combat this new threat. By this time, John had been promoted to wing commander and had taken over from Charles Appleton as CO of 604 Squadron. On return to Middle Wallop, with busy day and night operations, it was difficult for the night fighter crews to rest; the sector commander recognised the problem and billeted them at the Pheasant pub on the Salisbury road, the pub becoming the squadron's mess, staffed by members of the WAAF. It was totally self-contained, allowing the crews to sleep without interruption. John spent a year living there, while the married crew members had a house in Nether Wallop close to the airfield. When off duty, a favourite haunt was the Haunch of Venison in Salisbury, where there was good, home-cooked food, plus wine.

With the Luftwaffe heavily involved on the Eastern Front, operations at Middle Wallop were much reduced, allowing new tactics to be evolved and methods standardised. Many of the original Auxiliary Air Force personnel were replaced by aircrew from the Commonwealth and our allies, attracting highly competitive new talent.

John avoided publicity whenever possible and played down his 'cat's eyes' image as he was simply concentrating on the job. There was also a fundamental difference between the operation of the day fighter squadrons and those dedicated to night fighting. The commanding officers of the day fighter squadrons led from the front to engage with the enemy, as well as ground attack targets, in continual communication with his pilots. This was confirmed by the high-profile wing leaders, who led by personal example. At the end of the operational day, most were off duty and able to enjoy socialising until the next day's combat.

In contrast, John did not demonstrate his powers of leadership in the air with his colleagues behind him, but he and Jimmy, like the other night fighter crews, went off alone to seek out the enemy. John's leadership qualities were devoted to helping his crews improve their night-fighting expertise in the operation of the Beaufighter and the AI radar. He maintained contact with the specialist scientists to keep abreast of the latest developments.

The Beaufighter had a reputation for an engine failure on take-off to be fatal. When new crews arrived on 604 Squadron from the OTU (operational training unit), John would wedge them into his Beaufighter with Jimmy, taking off with four people aboard. He would reduce power on one engine as they crossed the boundary hedge and complete a circuit with one propeller slowly windmilling. He would then follow up with a take-off in formation with another Beaufighter and demonstrate an interception and attack, finishing with a steep-curved landing approach, with plenty of power available, allowing a good view below and behind, before flattening out for touchdown. These demonstrations were probably nerve-wracking for the novice crews, but John's comments were 'It's better to step out of the wreckage at the far end of the flare path than to be dug out at the threshold.' He was therefore able to demonstrate the versatility of Beaufighter operations in combat and created a keenness and confidence in the crews to become skilled in night fighting. Unlike day pilots, night fighter pilots had to fly on instruments, often in very poor weather conditions, with long periods of intense concentration, demanding special skills and technical training with no easy solutions.

When Jimmy was appointed navigation leader, he was also promoted to flight lieutenant; his duties in training the new crews were to fly with each in turn. With headphones plugged in, he stood behind the pilot and monitored practice interceptions, understanding the frustrations and emotions of the novice operators mastering the equipment. By this time, the aircrew status of the AI operators had been classified as observers (radio), with a new flying badge supplied with RO below a single wing, most of them carrying the rank of sergeant. There was no understanding why the letters had been reversed, but presumably, it was part of radar security.

John maintained close contact with the radar establishments to keep up with advances in technology and was able to advise on the practical applications or problems encountered, with Jimmy often accompanying him. During visits to the TRE, TFU, and FIU, John would often take along Derek Jackson, who was able to communicate in a practical way with the boffins. The Telecommunications Research Establishment (TRE) at Malvern was the originator of the equipment the Air Ministry specifications became practical equipment thanks to the top scientific brains in the country. The TRE had originally been at Worth Matravers on the south coast, but when a team of commandoes and radar experts were sent to France to learn about enemy radar systems, it was realised that a similar enemy raid could achieve knowledge of allied equipment.

Following the creation of the radar equipment at Malvern, it was taken to Defford where it was flight tested by the TFU (Telecommunications Flying Unit). Operational trials were carried out by the FIU based at Ford, where there were some highly qualified electronic engineers, and hand-picked night fighter crews on a rest tour. They tested and assessed the new equipment in the night fighters under operational conditions, with suggestions for improvements; John provided the latest knowledge of combat operations, confirming or challenging their conclusions.

The year 1941 had been highly successful for John and Jimmy, who were regarded as the best night fighting team, both having been promoted and awarded decorations. New hope was provided when on 7 December, Japan attacked Pearl Harbor, bringing the might of the USA into the war, together with reduced enemy air activity over Britain due to the German advances against the Soviet Union.

In the spring of 1942, intruder operations on both sides were developing, the aircraft of KGr 100 being equipped with new systems, which allowed blind bombing under the protection of solid cloud cover from take-off to return. These raiders were very difficult to locate and were largely immune to day fighters. They brought the night fighter force into action, even during daytime. The homing and blind flying aids had improved, the aircraft had a long endurance, and the AI radar was able to track targets in cloud.

On 23 May 1942, with low cloud covering the hills and going up to 20,000 feet, an attack from KGr 100 was planned. John was alerted and took off at 4 p.m., the ground vanishing as the undercarriage was retracted, with only the blind flying instruments to guide them through the ghostly vapour. Within a very short time, Starlight located a bandit and steered John and Jimmy towards it. As they climbed through the cloud layers, they were between layers when they spotted a He 111 only 1,000 yards ahead. Suddenly, the Heinkel went into a violent evasive turn to port, firing a broadside as they passed the Beaufighter about 100 yards to the side. John pulled rapidly round in a violent turn to follow, with the bandit vanishing into the cloud cover. Jimmy had difficulty in seeing the dim blip on his screen due to the bright ambient light and lost contact.

John called Starlight for more directions, the bandit having flown north near Shaftesbury. More vectors came from Starlight, continuing the chase. Suddenly, John saw the Heinkel again and began to close in with great determination. Jimmy realised it was going to be a demanding combat, put on his sunglasses to have a better chance of following the blip, and was just in time to see the Heinkel whip past with the guns blazing away into space. John held his ammunition until he was in lethal range. The enemy pilot straightened up in the belief that he had shaken off his pursuers and must have been amazed when John was able to get behind him after a few minutes. Without panicking, the enemy turned to attack with full power, but John was able to hold a turn inside the bandit, the turns becoming tighter and tighter under an enormous *g* force, making reading the instruments difficult.

Realising the Heinkel was unable to out-turn the Beaufighter, the German pilot resorted to twisting and turning, disappearing under John's wings and reappearing in the opposite direction at impossible angles. The Beaufighter vibrated with the strain and the engines roared under full power, with all the instruments gyrating. John then put his aircraft into a left bank to stabilise the operation, and Jimmy saw the Henkel flash past in a vertical dive; realising that they were getting very close to the ground, the enemy blip disappeared from Jimmy's radar and also Starlight. Both John and Jimmy were exhausted from all the manoeuvring and flew back to Middle Wallop after two and a half hours of violent combat, where they were told the Heinkel had hit high ground on Cranbourne Chase, having almost pulled out of the vertical dive; the pilot was the commanding officer of 7 Staffel of KGr 100. John had not fired a single shot during the entire combat. It was around this time that radar operators were designated as navigators, which was a more effective way of maintaining the secrecy of the AI systems while recognising their skills.

The Bomber Command offensive against Germany had been gradually increasing; in turn, the Luftwaffe retaliated with its night bombing of Britain, but instead of massed bombing, the German attacks were attempting to find any weaknesses in the RAF night defence by operating stealthy 'in and out' raids on coastal installations and carefully selected inland targets. The weakness in the GCI systems was the inability, as with most ground-based radar systems, to detect the low-flying raider until his final climb to bombing. The challenge was for the defending night fighter to be close enough to catch these hit-and-run bandits before they could quickly turn for home after dropping their bombs. In addition, the Germans had developed a jamming system that lost the target blips in a mass of interference towards the enemy coastline. This was a problem that only the boffins could help to counter.

In 1942, the Luftwaffe began to target Britain's cities of outstanding historic or artistic interest, as defined in the *Baedeker Guide*, which naturally became known as 'Baedeker Raids'. With bases in occupied France, the fast Do 217 bombers of the KG2 Bomber Wing were able to cause serious damage to these lightly defended non-industrial targets. To counter this low-level threat, a new AI Mk VII was developed with 4-inch (10-cm) wavelength radar, which replaced the fixed nose and wing-mounted antennas and sent out a powerful beam from a rotating nose-mounted transmitter with a tiltable parabolic dish reflector. This equipment was mounted in the nose of the Beaufighter, replacing the four 0.303-inch machine guns and protected by an electronically transparent radome.

The development of this AI had been over a long period. John first experienced it during the summer of 1941 in a flight from the SRDE (Signals R&D Establishment) at Christchurch. The new radar could track a target very low down at ranges of between 2 and 3 miles (3–5 km). Jimmy was pleased to find that the Beaufighter cannon ammunition belts had been connected in long belts, avoiding the previously difficult task of reloading heavy drums during violent manoeuvres. He found the new AI Mk VII completely different with all information displayed on a single tube. There was also less interference, the target seen clearly in a very limited beam.

While working up and gaining familiarity with the new equipment, both John and Jimmy were told they were tour expired and due a rest after three busy years of combat and pioneering night fighting. Bomber Command crews were usually tour expired after thirty missions, and fighter pilots were rested after eighteen months to two years. Long periods in the strain of combat caused 'operational fatigue' with a rest compulsory, although the hazards of operational training on 'rest' tours could be filled with danger.

3

Rest Tour and Mosquito Operations

John was posted to take over direction of the night fighter operational training units (OTUs) in Fighter Command, while Jimmy was allocated to 62 OTU at Usworth, but with John's influence, Jimmy was able to rejoin him at 81 Group, taking over from Rory Chisholm. They were both in effect grounded for six months, and just before leaving Middle Wallop, John was awarded a bar to his DSO, while Jimmy had reached the rank of squadron leader, had added a bar to his DFM, and was awarded a DFC.

No. 81 Group was located in a manor house in the Cotswold village of Avening, the site surrounded by huts. The atmosphere was totally different to squadron life, the house being isolated and looking gloomy, with many of the staff uncommunicative. John found it a rather difficult and unhappy period, and with his unfamiliarity with clerical duties, the paperwork was a burden. In contrast to their front-line duties, producing the correct report of a meeting and neatly keeping filing were priorities. Fortunately, the senior staff officer, Grp Capt. Robinson, a Battle of Britain veteran, understood the difficulties John was suffering, realising that John could make much more impact with OTU instructors and pupils through personal visits, rather than sitting behind a desk. Therefore, when John suggested he should make visits to the widely scattered training units, there was total agreement.

The three main night fighter OTUs were located at Cranfield in Bedfordshire, Charterhall in Berwickshire, and East Fortune near Edinburgh. The only practical way of making visits was by air. Initially, John and Jimmy used the group's Oxford, but soon John had persuaded 604 Squadron to lend him his Beaufighter. They were able to navigate around the country between beacons visiting the OTUs, where, following faultless approaches and short landing runs, he was able to advise and make suggestions based on his wide experience. Some of the instructors were obviously ineffective on the squadrons and dumped on the training units. John ensured they were posted, and he advised the squadrons that if they wanted good crews, they should send good instructors. Providing they performed well, they were guaranteed a return to their squadrons at the end of the six-month training period.

While John concentrated on raising pilot standards and finally crew operation, Jimmy was working on navigation training, with results showing gradual signs of improvement. However, the winter of 1942 was very bad, making training more demanding, with the result of increased accident rates. Although both John and Jimmy were not entirely happy with their task of improving training, they continued, but as time passed, they began making enquiries. With the end of the year approaching, there was still no news of a posting back to operations. At least they were able to keep in flying practice, but much of the work was routine, and they missed the challenges of combat.

As the end of January 1943 approached, John was able to break the good news to Jimmy that he had been given command of 85 Squadron, with Jimmy as navigation leader. Finishing their 'rest' period allowed them to get back into action. To John's delight, the squadron was equipped with Mosquito NF Mk IIs and based at Hunsdon in Hertfordshire, which was ideal for the defence of the London area. John and Jimmy drove to the officers' mess, a country house called Bonningtons, in his sports Lagonda, Jimmy following

John into the mess, where they were welcomed by a group of officers dressed in their best blue uniforms. A young pilot named Farrell introduced himself and offered John a drink, more an appeal than an invitation, because of the perceived mood. John asked for half a bitter, immediately relaxing the tension, the previous CO having strongly disapproved of drinking. Once John and Jimmy had started to get to know the crews, they began to check the overall squadron efficiency, but John was aware that he was probably going to lose some of his best pilots, when those from the Dominions would be segregated into their own squadrons. This was seen as a retrograde step, as the talent from around the world stimulated a healthy competitive spirit.

The first Mosquito NF Mk IIs were delivered to 85 Squadron in August 1942 and were fitted with a pilot indicator AI, which both John and Jimmy found inappropriate as it was important to share the interception duties between the two crew. Jimmy had difficulty checking out navigators in the air as there was only room for two in the cramped cockpit, so he had to rely on a ground trainer to assess the navigator's performance. While the squadron members were a dedicated group, they had become lazy due to insufficient action over a long period. Both John and Jimmy needed to sharpen up the crew's enthusiasm before they became targets of the Luftwaffe.

Hunsdon in Hertfordshire was a temporary wartime RAF station with only two runways and minimal accommodation. The airfield opened on 22 February 1941, and 85 Squadron moved in from Debden on 3 May. Many of the aircrew were billeted in surrounding villages, with John and the other pilots making lasting friendships with the local people. He had particularly fond memories of his time at Hunsdon sharing time with the local community. The Amiens prison raid, known as Operation Jericho, was flown from Hunsdon on 18 February 1944, led by Grp Capt. P. C. Pickard, who was killed on this operation. Flying ceased at Hunsdon on 16 May 1945, finally closing on 21 July 1947.

Following Mosquito familiarisation flights in daylight, John and Jimmy operated their first night practice flight. With their well-established technique, Jimmy controlled the early stages of the interception, and as they became close to the bandit, when it may take evasive action, John took over supported by Jimmy calling out the ranges. When the target was spotted visually, Jimmy helped John with additional information and instructions, freeing John from watching his own small cathode ray tube. Jimmy monitored the full interception picture on the screen mounted on the starboard side of the instrument panel.

They were both happy to be back in action, particularly flying the excellent Mosquito. John climbed up the narrow telescopic ladder through the side door, followed by Jimmy, into the cramped cockpit. While the pilot had a traditional seat, the navigator in effect sat on the top front of the wing main spar slightly behind the pilot. There was very little room for moving about and making use of maps and other navigation equipment. An advantage was that the Mosquito cockpit located between the radiators was comfortably warm even on cold nights, and Jimmy did not have to load the guns, of which there were four 0.303-inch machine guns in the nose of the NF Mk II and four powerful 20-mm cannon under the floor. In later Mosquito versions, the nose guns were replaced by the improved AI radar antenna protected by an electronically transparent radome.

In addition to being a navigator and operating the AI radar, the navigator was responsible for regulating the oxygen supply, fuel selector cocks, light switches, and other checklist tasks. Both crew spent much time familiarising themselves with the location of all the controls, so that in combat at night, they would have to locate them rapidly in the dark.

Ready to start their night familiarisation flight, John and Jimmy taxied to the runway threshold where John lined up and increased the power of the two mighty Merlins. As they roared along, the runway lights flashing past, the aircraft lifted away. John retracted the undercarriage, and the main wheels thumped into the nacelles, pulling the doors up behind them. They climbed to the east towards the North Sea, gaining height with the cockpit becoming warmer.

Jimmy was sweating in his full flying kit, pleasantly surprised that he was flying in a warm aircraft. The change from air-cooled engines in the Beaufighter to liquid-cooled Merlins in the Mosquito resulted in a significant increase in noise, and radiators in the wing leading edge crews had to remember that they were prone to damage from combat debris.

John and Jimmy had gained the impression that the night interception practices had been treated as routine with 'target' aircraft flown at a steady 10,000 feet. The instructions from the GCI controller provided a course to steer, but did not define a height. They heard their playmate 'target' being vectored after them, but with no heights mentioned. John said to Jimmy, 'I think we will have to shake these people up a bit'. John increased power and climbed rapidly to 20,000 feet, where he levelled out without any height instructions from the controller. The blip from the playmate on Jimmy's screen showed him behind and below, gradually becoming directly below John's Mosquito. The controller called that there must be contact, the two aircraft appearing to be together, but the playmate called out, 'definitely no joy'. The controller's response was 'then your weapon must be bent'.

John was amused, and called, 'Two Four calling, what are my angels?' After a brief silence, the controller responded, 'Angels ten', to which John replied, 'are you sure?' After another pause, the controller replied, 'well perhaps it is twelve'. John then advised him that he was at Angels 20, then appreciating that if there were not to be too few losses to the Luftwaffe, training would have to be more realistic.

It was not long before the Luftwaffe came over in strength. The squadron was scrambled on 3 March 1943, with Mosquitos chasing each other along the Hunsdon runway. John was too late to make contact with a GCI station, so he climbed out of the circuit, seeing active searchlights, with the anti-aircraft guns around the Thames estuary firing furiously. The searchlight batteries had been organised in box patterns around a series of evenly placed markers. Each fighter was allocated a box where he orbited until a target was illuminated by the lights or indicated by a cone of light where an AI signal may be picked up.

While orbiting in cloud, Jimmy picked up a potential bandit, getting to it as close as 500 feet, but John decided not to fire blindly as the chance of a hit was unlikely, and if they did hit it, they could be damaged by wreckage. It was also essential to visually identify the target as hostile, to avoid the destruction of an Allied aircraft. With reluctance, they abandoned the chase, but on returning to the marker beacon, Jimmy located another contact. John followed the target as it weaved its way home avoiding the searchlight beams, and John was able to identify a Do 217 twisting and turning ahead. They closed on the unsuspecting target, but when John pressed the firing button there was no reaction. They tried twice more, with no results, then the pilot of the Do 217 dived away and was lost in the ground echoes. On landing back at Hunsdon, it was found that an electric cable had broken, putting the gun firing circuit out of action.

It had been an unsuccessful night for 85 Squadron as a whole; three-quarters of the squadron flying eighteen sorties, and only John and Jimmy had located a bandit. Staff officers from Fighter Command visited Hunsdon to investigate the failure of the night's operations. While there, Jimmy mentioned a new improved version of the AI installed in the Beaufighters at Middle Wallop, which would be ideal for the detection of the low-flying, mine-laying bandits and the early-morning, low-level reconnaissance aircraft.

John was fully established in command, but he had some challenges, with experienced night fighting Canadian transferring to established RAF Canadian squadrons. There were also some incompetent crews and others who were willing, but operationally due a rest tour, putting 85 Squadron in need of reinforcements. John had maintained contact with good crews within his command, and 604 Squadron had been sent to Predannack on the Lizard in Cornwall. Many of the crew members who had served with John previously were more loyal to him when they returned to operations, rather than return to 604 Squadron. Another significant factor was that 85 Squadron was in the active front line, whereas

604 was in a quiet sector with little action. Night fighter crews were a relatively small group all knew each other, and John had a high level of influence in tracking down his most effective crews. With a few visits to OTUs and Fighter Command, John was able to attract some familiar pilots and navigators to join 85 Squadron.

He needed skilled and experienced crews to combat the fast-flying Do 217 raiders, which were coming in across the North Sea, bombing densely populated areas and escaping. In addition, the GCI stations had to be alert to detect these bandits in the short time available. Within a week of the unsuccessful 85 Squadron night operations, a travelling circus arrived equipped with Beaufighters and ground-training aids to brief the crews on the operation of the new centimetric wavelength Mk VIII AI radar, which could detect low-flying targets against ground clutter. The new system had a single clear display showing the direction and range of the target; it was a joint Anglo-American development. In late 1942, the first ninety-seven sets were delivered to Marshall's of Cambridge, where the old AI was removed together with 0.303-inch machine guns in the nose and replaced by a new antenna under a radome. The first conversion was DZ302, designated Mosquito NF XII, delivered to 85 Squadron in March 1943 and was soon adopted by the Cunningham/Rawnsley team for the rest of the year.

With the more potent Mosquito night fighters in service, the Luftwaffe began to send over very high-flying Ju 86R reconnaissance aircraft, which could be the precursor of high-flying bombers. One of the aircraft developed to combat this menace was a rapidly converted Mosquito Mk XV with extended wing span to allow operations of up to 48,000 feet. Six of these versions were adapted, the first one being a bomber version with a new nose scarfed on with the new AI radar installed, and a 20-mm cannon gun pack under the fuselage. John evaluated the new conversion against another Mosquito target and found the signals on the cathode ray tube were extremely clear with no sign of ground clutter. However, the enemy did not send over high-flying bombers as expected, meaning the high-altitude fighters were not required.

In April 1943, 85 Squadron was on parade for the formal presentation of the squadron crest, consisting of a hexagon which had been carried on SE.5a fighters in the Second World War. The motto was *Noctu diuque venamur*, which translated into 'We hunt by day and night'. The presentation was made by AVM Hugh 'Dingbat' Saunders, AOC 11 Group Fighter Command, who was highly regarded and later became Air Chief Marshal Sir Hugh Saunders.

On 13 May 1943, the squadron was moved from Hunsdon to the more permanent RAF station at West Malling in Kent close to Maidstone, putting 85 Squadron in the front line. The task was defending the famous Biggin Hill Sector, with plentiful enemy activity across the short Channel route on the south-east approaches to London. The airfield was grass with Sommerfield metal mesh along the main runway; it had been opened as an RAF station in June 1940, but had suffered considerable damage from Luftwaffe attacks during the Battle of Britain.

Instead of sending over high-altitude bombers, the Luftwaffe adapted the new Fw 190s as fast fighter bombers, carrying one large bomb, making day and night hit and run raids. The Hawker Typhoon had been developed for low-level air defence, with an advantage of speed and heavy armament, which were allocated to standing patrols along the south coast during the day, but at night, the raiders created a major challenge. The Fw 190s were small and difficult to locate, particularly after dropping fuel tanks and bombs, and able to return to base at very high speed. Previously, night fighting had depended on stealth, but it would need great skill and luck to catch these bandits. Their weak points were the Luftwaffe pilots who were inexperienced in night operations, and their Fw 190s had a short range, no radar, and a blind spot behind the tail.

The RAF squadron collected a kitty of cash and bottles to be awarded to the first crew to achieve success against these raiders, and on 16 May, only three days after arriving at West Malling, 85 Squadron was called to alert but held on the ground while Typhoons without the aid of radar were wondering around the sky with no success. After an hour of wasted effort, the sector controller ordered the Typhoons to land, scrambling 85 Squadron to attack the invading Fw 190s.

Peter Green, one of the flight commanders, together with navigator Grimstone, made contact with a returning Fw 190 positioning 3 miles behind as the enemy aircraft streaked home. Closing to within range, Peter shot him down as they crossed the coast at Dover. Then Geoff Howitt and George Irving investigated a searchlight cluster and made contact near Hastings. Although the Fw 190 pilot dived for home, the superior speed of the Mosquito allowed them to catch up and shoot him down before reaching the French coast. Bernard Thwaites and Will Clemo were recalled after chasing a bandit across the North Sea, but on the way back, they detected a returning raider, turned round rapidly, and blew it up from 50 yards astern. Some of the wreckage hit the Mosquito radiators, but they went after another raider which he fired at three times, causing debris to fly off, and was claimed as a probable hit. After being caught in searchlights, Shaw and Lowton detected a bandit near Gravesend, and when they fired, the target disintegrated, covering their windscreen in soot. This made four confirmed in one night plus one probable, and the crews celebrated following the success over what was believed to be an impossible target.

With West Malling being nearer the approaching bandits, standing patrols were maintained during the night, and as soon as GCI detected a build-up of enemy aircraft, the patrols were directed towards the coast, while a back-up scramble would be made from the home base to cover for any shortage of fuel with the aircraft in the air. John and Jimmy's first success on their second tour was not until 13 June, when they were on patrol off the Channel coast near Dungeness at 23,000 feet. With plenty of height in hand, the GCI station alerted John to a fast target approaching, and he flew towards the enemy aircraft.

Jimmy soon picked up the blip on his cathode ray tube only 1.5 miles ahead and well below. John increased power pulling round in a tight turn to catch what was a Fw 190 heading for London.

The blip closed gradually, the Mosquito gradually closing with this small high-speed target. The sector controller alerted the crews on the ground to advise that there was a Fw 190 approaching over West Malling with John close behind. As the combined engine noise came closer, John identified the raider visually as hostile and fired a brief burst. The target reared up, flicked over, and dived into the ground; the destruction was witnessed by the personnel on the ground. Surprisingly, the Luftwaffe pilot survived. When the aircraft flicked over, he was thrown out, pulling his parachute rip-cord; he was picked up by a searchlight crew.

Despite having performed in front of an audience twice, John's modesty with a rare combination of strength of character, integrity, and sense of purpose, together with a great sense of humour, meant he did not consider it more than just doing the job. When in command of an aircraft, his voice became crisp, impersonal and firm demonstrating his control of the situation. When dealing with people, he was a real gentleman with natural charm, from which everyone in contact with him benefited. These qualities carried through to his command of the squadrons, ensuring that the highest standards of efficiency were maintained and that everyone received the necessary training, especially with the newly developed radar equipment, by maintaining contact with the boffins. Leading by example ensured his crews attained the same standards.

The Germans soon realised that even the fast-operating Fw 190 nuisance raids were vulnerable and began to develop the Me 210, later to become the Me 410 with a pilot, gunner/navigator, and remote-controlled rearward-firing 13-mm heavy machine guns in blisters on either side of the fuselage. The crews at West Malling studied closely any intelligence gathered to determine the weak points of the aircraft defences.

In the summer of 1943, there were major changes in night fighter tactics, with improved and reliable AI radars, and a decision to use the earlier radar-equipped aircraft over enemy-occupied territory on offensive intruder operations, instead of being only on the defensive. Meanwhile, Luftwaffe raiders continued with a mix of difficult-to-intercept Fw 190s, Me 410s, and Ju 88s, flying into returning formations of RAF heavy bombers, making the identification by the GCI stations more challenging.

An innovation was the Ross night binoculars, which made recognition in the dark much easier, even down to the individual identity of the aircraft. During an enemy raid on Portsmouth in mid-August, John and Jimmy were able to identify two Beaufighters and a Mosquito without difficulty. In addition, they both made regular visits to the Fighter Interception Unit, Defford, Sector Operations, Group, and Fighter Command to keep up to date with the latest equipment and operational requirements. During this time, they assessed the new US-developed AI Mk X, which was later introduced into combat operations by 85 Squadron.

The skies over Britain and occupied Europe were becoming increasingly congested, with massed USAAF day bomber formations going out in the mornings, returning often after dusk. As darkness fell the RAF heavy bomber streams began their night raids, but they were suffering appalling losses. RAF losses on one raid were over 500 aircrew, more than the total losses in the Battle of Britain.

On the night of 8 September 1943, seven Luftwaffe fighter bombers came over Britain. Three were destroyed by 85 Squadron, including John's nineteenth success, but with some hazards. GCI vectored the Mosquito to the north as a wave of enemy bombers came across. Jimmy picked up a contact east of North Foreland, giving chase at 22,000 feet. The night was very dark, making the target difficult to see. Jimmy brought John closer and the blip was coming to the minimum range of 800 feet. John believed he had picked up the glow of the bandit's exhaust, approaching 600 feet range. With a very indistinct sighting, John asked Jimmy to view it through the Ross night binoculars, bringing the Fw 190 into clear vision, with underwing fuel tanks and a bomb below the fuselage.

John fired and the two fuel tanks were jettisoned passing under the Mosquito wings. The enemy pilot weaving gently and apparently unaware that John was 30 feet below, continuing on his course. Following stealthily behind, John eased back and came up for another shot, with hits seen on the fuselage. The Fw 190 slowed down and started to weave. John dropped down below the enemy aircraft into his blind spot, slowly manoeuvring back. Looking through the night vision device, Jimmy saw that the bomb was still carried and just above their cockpit. However, John had manoeuvred into a safe position, ready for another attack, moving up for the third time as close as 75 yards, once again firing, causing a bright flash and the enemy cockpit coming away, with debris passing the Mosquito.

Suddenly, the cockpit was filled with white smoke from behind John's seat, out of the cabin heater, and engine coolant pouring out, signifying a hit in the radiator. John immediately stopped the Merlin and feathered the propeller, trimming the aircraft for single-engine flight, and called for an emergency heading as they crossed the coast and headed for home. John was worried about the indicated height as instead of the expected 15,000 feet, the altimeter was showing only 5,000 feet, heading back over the Thames estuary at its narrowest point to avoid balloons and AA guns. Then as they approached West Malling, there was a ring of searchlights, and the red beacon of the airfield was illuminated. John joined a right-hand circuit on the good engine and made a light-as-a-feather landing, to be told the Fw 190 was confirmed as crashing in the sea off Aldeburgh.

With the strain of the latter combat, it was therefore welcome when John announced he was taking a few days of leave, although he would never admit to being combat-weary. He travelled by train to St Ives to stay with his uncle at Phillack on the rugged Atlantic coast, which was an ideal retreat with the beaches and moorland close by. Jimmy took the train to Windemere, where he enjoyed the peace of the Cumberland fells. His wife, Micky, had been an ambulance driver and then joined the ATS (Auxiliary Territorial Service), which made it almost impossible for them to take leave at the same time.

Soon after their return from leave, on 1 October, a Wellington flying classroom arrived to instruct in the operation of AI Mk

X. The Luftwaffe also began operations with the improved Ju 188s, and by the end of the first week in October, the squadron experienced its busiest night for a long time. The bandits came over in three waves of mixed aircraft, with fifteen in the first, thirty in the second, and twelve in the last. Although Jimmy was having trouble with the AI that night, as they were returning to base, he detected a faint echo on one side of the cathode ray tube (CRT), alerting John of the possibility of a target. As Jimmy was speaking, the target flashed by in front at almost the same height, and John turned tightly to position about 200 yards behind, dropping down below as usual.

Using his night glasses, Jimmy identified it as a Ju 188. John pulled up to get the bandit into his line of fire. Unfortunately, the enemy crew were alert and before John could fire, the under gunner fired straight back into their faces with three 13-mm rounds coming through the top left corner of the laminated windscreen, close to John's head. The windscreen was completely opaque and John fired blindly, moving the nose around in the hope of achieving a lucky hit.

There was no sign of the enemy aircraft through the side windows, and John slowed down to reduce wind pressure and Jimmy put on his parachute in case the windscreen collapsed. John had collected a face full of glass shards. Jimmy lent John his goggles as added protection. John called for an emergency homing to base, crossing back across the coast and making a curved approach for a gentle landing.

They were met by concerned personnel and taken to sick quarters where the MO removed fragments of Perspex from John's face with tweezers, one piece embedded within a fraction of an inch from his left eye. Jimmy was shaking fragments from his clothing, and recovering from the shock of the encounter, by which time the last of the raiders were on their way home. Soon after this incident, Jimmy became the first radar navigator to be awarded the Distinguished Service Order (DSO), although as he felt he was not performing as well as he might, he did not feel he deserved it.

In mid-1943, the Luftwaffe began to use the fast and elusive Ju 188 and Me 410 to attract defending RAF fighters while other enemy aircraft slipped through towards the intended targets. The squadron crews found when they attempted to intercept these aircraft, they took violent evasive action and dived for home, keeping the Mosquito night fighters busy. The reason was soon established when a recently shot down German crew were interrogated and it was established that the aircraft were fitted with a rearward-facing radar, alerting the crew to RAF night fighters. The Mosquito had a speed advantage over the Ju 188, but the Me 410 flew at a similar speed to the Mosquito, giving the tail-mounted radar a definite advantage.

However, the squadron continued to achieve successes with the fiftieth night victory in November when an Fw 190 was destroyed by a crew who had been with John on 604 Squadron, and returned for a second tour on 85 Squadron. With other experienced crews moving on to command new night fighter squadrons, John was always on the lookout for new experienced crews on their second tour.

With the approach of winter, bad weather returned with long nights and low temperatures, when diving from altitude after a bandit, windscreens could ice over, and the overworked Merlins were becoming tired. The rear radar-fitted German aircraft were a challenge to catch, particularly as they tended to come over on moonless nights when they could not be detected visually. With the introduction of the American AI Mk X radar in Mosquito NF Mk XVIIs, operational trials had to be conducted before they could be used in combat. It was also apparent that the existing Mosquitos were becoming worn out, an example for John on a routine patrol in December when the controls became very sluggish and the aircraft tended to roll to the left.

On visual inspection, it was noticed the port flap was stuck up in the opposite direction to normal. John carefully returned to base and landed fast without selecting the flaps. The ground crew found the inner section of the flap was only held on by the remains of one hinge. Just over a week later in bitterly cold mid-December, the port engine began to vibrate violently, causing John to switch it off and feather the propeller. John maintained height until he was sure of being able to glide back to West Malling; when he alerted the controller, the reply was that the weather was good and a 'canopy' of searchlights would be lit up as guidance. John began a gentle glide, allowing a straight-in landing without the customary circuit. However, as the airfield was approached, the visibility became worse and when down to 600 feet, the lights could not be seen. John called to confirm that a snowstorm had arrived over the airfield.

By this time, they were too low to abandon the aircraft and were unable to climb over high ground towards Ford, their nearest diversion. Having studied all the alternatives, John elected to try for Ford, but just as he set course, Jimmy looked back and saw the West Malling lights through a gap in the cloud in line with the flarepath. John turned back to starboard and dived through the gap surrounded by thick cloud on both sides and above, touching down at high speed, finishing up at the far end of the landing ground, but was unable to taxi on one engine. The ground crew had difficulty locating the stranded Mosquito in the snow storm, and finally Jimmy dropped out of the crew door to the grass below and fired Very cartridges, attracting attention at last.

The service introduction of the new AI Mk X radar was a challenge, particularly with getting accustomed to the new controls. It was discovered that most of the controls could be preset during a night-flying test, although there were still a number that had to be located rapidly by touch. The radar information display was totally different to anything in the past. The configuration was a pair of tubes framed in rectangle masks with the blips appearing at ranges of up to 10 miles as small rectangle blobs on the right-hand tube, allowing a range and bearing to be read and relative course determined for the target. A blip was then selected and transferred to the left-hand tube, which displayed it as a large vertical clock face ahead of the fighter. This allowed the radar operator to guide the pilot using clock references. The scanner rotated about a vertical axis through 180 degrees from beam to beam, nodding as it rotated allowing detection above and below the fighter's line of sight. The angular limit could be varied by the operator to reduce ground echoes at low level or following evasion at close range.

New Mosquitos were also fitted with additional radar equipment under the canopy behind the pilot's seat, allowing guidance from ground-based radar beacons, installed all over the country, making the aircraft independent of ground control for position fixings and homings. Although the new equipment was a challenge, Jimmy felt that it would be possible to operate with some success without reference to ground control. This would allow the RAF to go on the offensive and combat the Luftwaffe over their own territory. As navigation leader, Jimmy had to ensure that the new radar operators did not hesitate when a target was detected, avoiding the long chase, rapidly moving into minimum range. With the RAF undergoing the most rapid expansion in its history, new aircrew were coming from a wide variety of educations and backgrounds, with Jimmy having to adapt to the capabilities of lively modern minds, while at the same time becoming proficient on the new equipment himself and fully support John in combat.

There had been a quiet period over Christmas, but on 2 January 1944, action recommenced. While still using the Mk VIII radar in their old Mosquito, they were patrolling over the Channel at 25,000 feet, and control advised of a potential target approaching fast from the south-east. The controller brought them around, and much to Jimmy's delight, a target appeared on his tube. With little height advantage available, the bandit began to take violent yet predictable evasive action. When they were some 3,000 feet behind, John caught sight of the target's exhaust, but the bandit must have sensed he was being followed, making a steep turn to the left and diving with constant weaving.

John selected the recently installed nitrous oxide boost and the Mosquito accelerated forward, closing the gap between the aircraft over the Channel. As the French coast approached, the bandit must have assumed he was safe easing off on his manoeuvring and slowing down. The target blip came to the ideal position on the tube—at 20 degrees at twelve o'clock, range 1,200 reducing to 1,000 yards, by which time John had a visual, confirming it as a Me 410. As they came close to the French coast, John pulled up the nose and fired his cannons, hitting the enemy aircraft and sending it down in flames. The aircraft was confirmed by the Royal Observer Corps (ROC), crashing between Le Tourquet and Berck at 11.59 p.m., with John having fired only ten rounds.

This was to be the twentieth and last success for John as a few weeks later, he was promoted to group captain and posted to a staff position at HQ 11 Group in charge of night operations—one of the youngest group captains in the RAF at twenty-six years old. Jimmy was offered the opportunity of staying with 85 Squadron, crewing with another pilot, following eight years with John as a legendary team. John and Jimmy were totally different characters, but blended well in their partnership. John's professionalism in the air was fully supported by Jimmy. John's background was practical and probably close to upper middle class, while Jimmy was thirteen years older and married. Jimmy had qualified as an electrical engineer and aged thirty-two was only 5 feet 3.5 inches and 105 lb. Both men were very practical and had started their service as volunteers with the Auxiliary squadrons, giving John the opportunity to fly and Jimmy to achieve aircrew status. While John was undertaking his peacetime duties as chief test pilot at Hatfield, he and Jimmy maintained regular contact until Jimmy died in 1965.

As well as being very professional in the air, John also knew how to party. When he was awarded the second bar to his DSO and about to depart for his duties at Fighter Command, the squadron provided a memorable farewell party starting at midday. His colleagues were determined to get John 'under the table' and he responded with his regular half pint of beer, but mysteriously his tankard kept getting topped with neat gin until it was a clear liquid. John rose to the challenge and by 3.30 p.m. had finished it. In total command, but perhaps a little flushed, he said sleep was called for, returning to his accommodation. To the delight of the squadron, he returned to the mess at just after 6 p.m., ready to continue the party, looking as immaculate as ever.

With Wing Commander C. M. Miller as the new CO of 85 Squadron performing well, Jimmy was dubious of teaming up with a new pilot, although he was reluctant to break up from his friends and became navigation leader in name alone, with new talent available to take his place operationally. He therefore took a posting to the FIU at Ford, where his partnership with John lapsed for a while.

In March 1944, while John was on staff duties at Uxbridge, Air Marshal Sir Roderick Hill asked him to go to Farnborough with Group Captain 'Sailor' Malan to evaluate the new de Havilland Vampire jet fighter. John's task was to check the Vampire out for its suitability as a night fighter; Malan's role was to check it as a day fighter. This was a significant event for John as it was his introduction to the new era of jet aviation, designed by the company where he had his early engineering training and test flying experience. Major Frank Halford was the company engine designer and pioneered the production of the world's first production jet engine, to power a fighter, the engine becoming the de Havilland Goblin. The chief designer, R. E. Bishop, and his team designed the diminutive Vampire around the engine with its twin tail boom configuration to maintain the greatest efficiency with the available thrust.

John was familiar with climbing into the cockpits of Beaufighters and Mosquitos, so the single-seat cockpit of the Vampire with its nose wheel undercarriage which was close to the ground but with excellent all-round visibility was a new experience. It was basically a simple aircraft that John enjoyed flying. He advised that with additional endurance and accommodation for a navigator, it would be ideal as a night fighter. On his return to civilian test flying, John was to be responsible for managing the flight development of the Vampire night fighter and the later Venom night fighter.

Fighter Command reverted to its pre-war title of Air Defence of Great Britain (ADGB), to differentiate from the newly formed Allied Tactical Air Force (TAF) to support the invasion of Europe. The

ADGB was commanded by Air Marshal Sir Roderick Hill, and the most vital front-line 11 Group was commanded by AVM 'Dingbat' Saunders. John was heavily involved in the preparation for the planned Allied invasion, in particular the night fighting force, and although it involved an enormous amount of paperwork, he was happy to labour through it, facing the enormous challenge as the invasion of Nazi Europe became a reality.

It soon became obvious that there was a need for someone to make rapid tours of the night fighter stations, to report on conditions, effectiveness, and morale, as well as note any complaints. With the squadrons moving around so often, the situation changed daily. John therefore made arrangements to bring Jimmy back into the team, and he found a high level of enthusiasm among the crews who wanted to get started. There were still spasmodic enemy night raids along the south coast against assembly areas, with seventeen night fighter and intruder squadrons to counter these raids. The Luftwaffe lost at least twenty-two aircraft and crews. There was a total of 171 Allied day fighter and fighter bomber squadrons packed in the south-east of England, ready to undertake the duties of the 2nd TAF (Tactical Air Force).

In the build-up of preparations for the invasion, a number of well-defended and camouflaged launch sites of the flying pilotless V-1 flying bomb were attacked. They were located along Pas-de-Calais and towards Cherbourg. Difficult to catch due to their small size and high speed, the 'Doodlebugs' did not begin operations until a week following D-Day on 6 June 1944.

John had his first opportunity to inspect the narrow strip of French coast on 9 June when he flew with 96 Squadron, based at West Malling, with Jimmy. They climbed in their Mosquito directed by one of the new Fighter Direction Tenders and saw some ground fires burning in the Caen area. They were directed to some low-flying bandits attacking shipping, but Jimmy was unable to maintain contact. They were then vectored unsuccessfully to another contact with the ship's guns firing haphazardly at any engine sound, resulting in John deciding to call it a night and return to base.

On 1 May 1944, 85 Squadron was transferred from ADGB to 100 Group in Bomber Command, moving from West Malling to Swannington in Norfolk equipped with Mosquito NF Mk XVIIs, a new role to provide long-range night fighter escorts for RAF heavy bomber raids. The plan was to infiltrate into the bomber streams on their way to attack targets in Germany and catch the enemy night fighters as they attempted to shoot down the bombers. There was always the risk that the RAF bomber rear gunners might shoot down the Mosquitos in error. The squadron crews were delighted to move from defensive to offensive operations, but the navigators required additional training to adapt them to long-range night flying. While the training was going on, the V-1 offensive began on 13 June and the squadron was sent back to West Malling on 21 July to help counter the new threat of flying bombs.

John was concerned about using Mosquitos against flying bombs as the wing leading edge radiators were vulnerable to the debris from the explosion when the V-1 was hit. One example was when a crew had to abandon their aircraft when the nose of their Mosquito was split open, though the same crew later accounted for the destruction of thirty-one flying bombs. With Tempests and other fighters having improved success at destroying flying bombs, 85 Squadron returned to Swannington on 29 August, re-equipping with NF Mk XXXs in November. The crews were able to gain high scores during their bomber support duties.

Meanwhile, John was able to make visits to the night fighter squadrons based both in Britain and Europe as the advances from Normandy progressed, operating faster versions of Mosquito. Many of the crews had been trained by John and Jimmy, the two of them being a major contribution to building the structure of the RAF night fighter force. As group captain night operations throughout the Allied invasion of Europe, John was fully involved with supporting the squadrons as they advanced, maintaining contact with the action right up to the end of the war in Europe on 8 May 1945.

John was then posted on attachment to Asia, with plans to form a group in Rangoon, including a Mosquito squadron to recover Singapore from the Japanese. John was to take Jimmy with him to oversee Mosquito operations, although he would not fly them in action. John flew a new Mosquito out to a maintenance unit at Allahabad in India, to exchange it for a fully modified example with all the vital operational equipment. They departed from Portreath in Cornwall, flying via Malta, Cairo, and Baghdad to Karachi. While flying from there to Allahabad in August 1945, they learned that with the dropping of the atomic bombs, Japan had surrendered and the Second World War was over.

With the Japanese general arriving in Rangoon to surrender to Air Marshal Saunders, the war was over for John and he asked his AOC whether, being on detachment from 11 Group, he could return home. However, Rangoon was under the control of South East Asia Command, which was headquartered in Ceylon, from where he would have to obtain permission to depart. John and Jimmy flew in a Sunderland flying boat as passengers to Ceylon, where the climate was very comfortable. Upon going to the mess for dinner, he met with surprise Air Marshal Sir Ralph Cochrane, by then AOC-in-C Transport Command, who kindly offered John and Jimmy a flight back to Britain the next day.

Although John had been offered a permanent commission in the RAF, he was aware that he could return to de Havilland as a test pilot, where he would continue his love of flying, which he certainly would not achieve in the RAF. John was ready to return to an organisation that had expanded out of all recognition during the seven years he had been away. By then, it was known as the de Havilland World Enterprise, encompassing aircraft, engine, and propeller companies in Britain as well as all the overseas interests. Employee numbers during the war years had risen from 5,000 to 38,000 globally, with even greater numbers involved in the overall supply chain. Turnover had risen from £1.5 million to over £25 million during the last year of the war, not including the government-owned shadow factories and de Havilland-associated companies at home and abroad. Among the production totals were 7,781 Mosquitos, over 8,000 Tiger Moths, and 8,750 Airspeed Oxfords, in addition to a total of well over 100,000 propellers—more than any other company.

The de Havilland Aircraft Company had entered the jet age in 1943 with the Vampire powered by a de Havilland Engine Company Goblin turbo jet, giving many opportunities for John to be involved in all aspects of jet aviation development. With much competition for flying jobs from experienced aircrew, John was fortunate that as he had been a de Havilland test pilot before the war, and by law, he was entitled to return to his job if he wished. John finished the war as a highly decorated senior officer with an outstanding combat record, although he disliked the publicity associated with his achievements.

4

Return to de Havilland

When the Second World War finally ended, Britain was effectively bankrupt. A mere forty-five years before, at the start of the twentieth century, it had been one of the most powerful countries in the world, but having fought two world wars in the space of thirty years, the once invincible Commonwealth was breaking up and Britain continued to endure wartime austerity. Rationing continued for some years after the end of the war, and in the author's experience, visiting Berlin in 1947, where there was still bomb rubble beside the roads and wrecked trains alongside the railway lines, I enjoyed a cream chocolate éclair for the first time. Even then I was old enough to wonder who had won the war.

Although bombed during the war, Britain did not suffer the massive destruction experienced by Germany, but it shared some of the advantages offered by the new post-war world. Aviation had made significant improvements in technology over the six years from 1939 and nowhere more dramatically than in Germany. During the war, improvements in aircraft design allowed them to reach speeds of up to 500 miles an hour, but it was apparent that the handling of the aeroplanes changed when nearing the speed of sound, then known as the sound barrier. Buffeting and problems with control at high subsonic and transonic speeds suggested that the aerodynamics of high-speed aircraft were changing. These changes in aerodynamics included thinner, swept-back wings, and experiments were conducted with revolutionary configurations, particularly airframes with delta wings, often without conventional horizontal tailplanes and elevators to control pitch.

Jet and rocket engines provided more advanced forms of power, although initially, it was of reduced efficiency. Flying long distances had become commonplace during the war, particularly over the Atlantic. In Britain and the United States, even during the war, there was a recognition that passenger air travel, mainly for the wealthy, offered opportunities once the war was over. It presented the possibilities of a golden age for British aviation. The immediate post-war years brought an increased interest in aviation. The annual Farnborough air shows provided a venue in which British aircraft companies like de Havilland, Hawker, Gloster, Avro, and the others could display their latest designs. The test pilots, many of whom were accomplished wartime pilots, became public heroes. Despite the difficulties of the recovery, the future for aviation looked bright and optimistic.

In 1944, when Captain de Havilland was knighted for services to aviation, working as part of the Brabazon Committee, his company studied a design for a jet airliner based on the twin boom shape of its jet-powered Vampire fighter, which flew as a prototype in 1943. Over the following four years, the concept changed from a tailless layout to accommodate more passengers in an aircraft with swept-wings. The project, DH.106, became known as the Comet. However, before the design could be finalised, research was needed to understand the aerodynamic and structural problems of such revolutionary concepts.

At the end of the war, John Cunningham was a celebrated and successful RAF pilot. A bright career undoubtedly awaited him in the RAF, but this was not what he wanted. The de Havilland Aircraft Company was very much a family affair. It was founded in September 1920 by Geoffrey de Havilland, who had been designing and flying aeroplanes for some ten years. He had the foresight to see that, with the cancellation of many military contracts, the 1920s would present opportunities in the civil market. The company designed and sold many successful aircraft, both for the local airline operators and for the enthusiastic aviators who could afford to indulge themselves in flying. Well-known types were the family of Moth light aeroplanes including the 1930s Tiger Moth, which became the basic *ab initio* trainer of the RAF before, during, and after the Second World War. Larger types included the DH.84 Dragon, which could be operated without subsidies at a profit on local services, later to be developed into the improved DH.89 Dragon Rapide.

Geoffrey married Louie Thomas in 1909, and over the years, they had three sons—Geoffrey Raoul, Peter, and John, who all inherited their father's enthusiasm for flying and worked with him in the company as test pilots. Sadly, as is the way with aviation, and in particular with test flying, lives were lost. On 23 August 1943, John was killed when the Mosquito he was flying collided with another being flown by George Gibbins. All four crew members died. Geoffrey Raoul was already the chief test pilot of the company and was the first to fly many of the prototypes. He was a skilled and competent pilot with attention to detail so essential for testing work. He was also a charming, typically English gentleman, smartly dressed in blazer and slacks, and always game for a party or the arm of a pretty girl, but not always easy to work with.

John Cunningham was demobilised in November 1945 and rejoined de Havilland at Hatfield on 1 December, at the age of twenty-eight, on an annual salary of £1,500, enough for him to be financially comfortable. He was appointed chief test pilot of the de Havilland Engine Company, working closely with Geoffrey de Havilland Jnr, leader of the Aircraft Company test flying team. He lived with his mother and sister, Mary, in a period country house at Kinsbourne Green, just north of Harpenden in Hertfordshire, where he could indulge in his enjoyment of the surrounding countryside. With his mother looking after his domestic needs, he was able to concentrate on his new demanding test flying tasks at Hatfield.

On his return to the company that he had visited only briefly since 1939, he knew many people still there. The 'family' spirit was very evident, and Sir Geoffrey de Havilland welcomed John back to the old company. Although it had been very busy during the war, the organisation was now expanding into the jet age and all its challenges. With speeds of new aircraft almost double those of Second World War combat types, there were greater risks with increased stresses and fatigue, resulting in a number of test pilots losing their lives while pushing the boundaries into the unknown. John always emphasised that test pilots do not do the job for financial gain, and rates of pay in aviation were not high when compared with other industries. With the pioneering attitude of the long-serving de Havilland personnel at Hatfield, and the family atmosphere, the appeal of flying compensated for the lower rates of pay.

At the beginning of 1946, John was asked by the Air Ministry to reform his old 604 Auxiliary Squadron, which was equipped with Spitfires. Although he did not participate in flying operations, he was able to locate the pilots required, and after a year was able to withdraw back to his duties at Hatfield. The flying workload was very high with demands on both John and his team, consisting of the experienced Pat Fillingham, Geoffrey Pike, and Jack Greenland. Pat and Geoffrey had been students of the Tech School, like John. John also needed a pilot to handle the DH.108 test flying, and John Derry, who was working for Supermarine, appeared suitable. Rather than approaching Derry direct, John visited Jeffrey Quill, chief test pilot of Supermarine, and asked if Derry was available. Jeffrey was delighted to help as he had no suitable project for Derry and was happy to release him to join the de Havilland team at Hatfield, where his obvious talents would be more appreciated.

Just over two months before John rejoined the company, the commander in chief of the Royal Swedish Air Force (RSAF) had visited Hatfield to evaluate the DH Goblin-powered Vampire jet fighter, resulting in a contract being signed on 9 February 1946 for an initial batch of Vampire F.1s, including the Goblin jet engines, followed later by license production of Goblin 3 engines for the RSAF for later fighters designed by SAAB. This was the first large export order for the British aircraft industry, and on 4 June 1946, the first five aircraft departed Hatfield on the delivery flight, the overall total in two orders was for seventy Vampires.

John's tasks were to continue flight development of the 3,000-lb thrust Goblin and commence the initial testing of the more powerful 5,000-lb thrust Ghost. John was also involved in the introduction of the Vampires to Sweden, and with his vast experience in night fighter operations, he was asked to advise on the radar support and to operate the new jet fighters. The use of radar defence in Britain was still classified, but the head of military intelligence allowed the release of information by John, particularly as Britain was in desperate need of export earnings. John spent nearly a month in the frozen wastes of Sweden in his new much wider role as an international consultant, pilot, and ambassador. His natural modesty and charm, backed by his professionalism, made a great impact on the Swedes.

Soon after, a sale was made to Switzerland with an initial evaluation batch of four F.1s, the first of which, J-1001 was delivered by John on 27 September 1946 to Geneva. He took off at the same time as Geoffrey de Havilland Jnr, who was flying the experimental DH.108 prototype TG306 in the transonic region. Geoffrey was investigating the effects of the speed of sound on aircraft, popularly known as 'Breaking the Sound Barrier'. On arriving in Geneva, John was having breakfast the following day when he saw the headlines in the local newspaper: 'Test Pilot Geoffrey de Havilland is Missing'. Captain de Havilland called John later in the day and asked John to return as soon as was reasonable, when he had done all that was required.

When John had returned to Hatfield after the war, the company was busy with the development of the planned Comet jet airliner programme, as well as the challenges of supersonic flight. The

DH.108 was a tailless experimental jet powered by a single Goblin with new metal swept-back wings fitted to a wooden fuselage pod of a Vampire, along with a single swept-back fin and rudder. The aircraft was intended to investigate the aerodynamics of the Comet and future jet fighter design. Geoffrey de Havilland Jnr had made the maiden flight of the low-speed prototype TG283 from the long runway at RAF Woodbridge on 15 May 1946, soon returning to Hatfield where he continued development trials investigating handling and aerodynamics of tailless flight.

It was the second DH.108 prototype that Geoffrey de Havilland Jnr was flying on 27 September, and he felt certain that the aircraft was capable of exceeding the existing world speed record, which then stood at 616 mph, achieved by 'Teddy' Donaldson in an RAF Meteor. He therefore planned to practise before going to the Tangmere base for the speed record along the south coast instrumented course. While flying over the Thames Estuary, the small aircraft encountered turbulence, which resulted in structural failure and the loss of the pilot. The wreckage fell near Egypt Bay in Kent. Geoffrey Jnr had often referred to the aircraft he was testing as 'boilers' and knew the risks he was taking.

John was sad to have lost his friend, but he had become used to such situations during the war when many of his comrades were lost. The need like all test pilots was to carry on. With two brothers lost in test flying accidents, the third brother, Peter, gave up test flying and took up a role in sales. Ironically on the evening of the accident, Sir Geoffrey de Havilland had cleared the final specification of the Comet programme with BOAC, allowing detail design to begin.

On John's return from Geneva, Sir Geoffrey asked him to become chief test pilot, taking charge of all de Havilland test flying at Hatfield with the aircraft, engine and propeller companies, and also test flying from Christchurch and Hurn, Leavesden, and Hawarden near Chester. John was paid the same as Geoffrey Jnr at £2,000 a year and had a team of over twenty test pilots working for him. He needed to have the right people in the right place and the right tasks, which resulted in some departing and the employment of new talent to build a team of balanced personalities, a task he was familiar with during his wartime service. It was interesting that few of the team were graduates of the Empire Test Pilots' School (ETPS), and they all operated with simple private pilots' licences (PPL), which years later were converted into special commercial licences, as they were all earning their living test flying.

John had a great deal of respect and admiration for the de Havilland family, and Geoffrey was buried quietly in Tewin churchyard next to his brother John.

Meanwhile, John had to become fully aware of the de Havilland World Enterprise's diverse and huge design, development, and production programmes, the export market booming with Vampires selling worldwide. Geoffrey de Havilland had been exploring the performance and handling of the DH.108 approaching the speed of sound. John's first daunting task was to fly the surviving low-speed DH.108 to establish what had caused the death of Geoffrey, a programme which took the aircraft to its fine limits, without going too far. Geoffrey had been the only pilot to fly the DH.108, and John made his first flight in TG283 on 18 October 1946.

A third DH.108 VW120 was ordered for high-speed research and featured a more pointed nose and pressure cabin. John made the maiden flight from Hatfield on 24 July 1947. On the same day he made the first flight of the new DH.108, he also made the first flight of Ghost 50 engine test-bed Lancastrian VM703 with C. D. Beaumont of the de Havilland Engine Company in preparation for the Comet. John conducted Ghost engine performance testing up to heights of 35,000 feet in an unpressurised wartime vintage Lancaster bomber conversion, which was demanding environmentally but regarded as routine by John.

John was making two or three flights a day in the two DH.108s, and by the end of 1947, he had over 100 flights recorded. The flight test schedule was variable and included stalls with an anti-spin parachute fitted. His seventh DH.108 flight on 31 October 1946 in the low-speed TG283 is covered in his own words in Chapter 8. His other tests included the effects of power controls, accelerations at 35,000 feet, cockpit temperatures, and calibration and *g* turns. Between them the two Johns, Cunningham and Derry made 294 DH.108 test flights from 1946 to 1950, with Cunningham making 163 and Derry 131.

Sir Geoffrey de Havilland wanted John to concentrate on the Comet flight development programme, and John Derry was assigned to share testing of the DH.108. As a result of the flight testing of all three DH.108s, a tailless configuration was found to be unsuitable for the Comet due to centre of gravity limitations and lack of stability in pitch, but the aerodynamics of the swept-wing assisted greatly in the development of the DH.110, later to become the Sea Vixen naval strike fighter.

John Derry flew DH VW120 on the 100-km international closed-circuit speed record on the evening of 12 April 1948, setting up a new speed of 605.23 mph over a pentagonal course near Hatfield. On 9 September, the same pilot with the same aircraft exceeded the speed of sound for the first time outside America while in a dive from 40,000 feet, completely losing control, but regaining it at 30,000 feet when the Mach number had reduced in denser air. A few days later, John Derry repeated the supersonic dive. Both surviving aircraft were passed on to the RAE at Farnborough once their testing at Hatfield was complete, but sadly both were lost, killing their pilots.

The first pilot to exceed the speed of sound was American Major Chuck Yeager in the rocket-powered Bell X-1 carried aloft under a converted B-29 bomber and landing unpowered back at Edwards Air Force Base

Cunningham said later, unsurprisingly, that he could sense the inherent instability of the aeroplane and that it would not take much to upset it. He tried to reproduce the conditions when Geoffrey de Havilland Jnr had been killed by increasing speed incrementally at higher altitudes. He found little damping of pitch, and at relevant Mach and ASI, small changes made the aeroplane unstable.

More than a year after Geoffrey's crash, while trying to recreate the conditions that had killed him, John Derry found that when descending gently, passing through 4,500 feet with a Mach number of 0.875 and a speed of 625 mph, a patch of bumpy air apparently induced an extremely violent and uncontrollable pitching oscillation with a sustained cycle of +4 to -3 g several times a second. Immediately closing the throttle, when the Mach number reduced to 0.85, the aircraft once again flew smoothly. It was concluded that this severe oscillation was the cause of the accident resulting in Geoffrey being thrown up against the canopy, breaking his neck and causing structural failure. No fault was found with the engine.

John had gained much operating experience with military aircraft, where performance and manoeuvrability were paramount. Although the rules of flight were identical, the principles of operating a commercial airliner were totally different—economy and passenger comfort were essential. Events in Britain had been followed with interest in American aircraft companies, and in December 1946, Cunningham spent some time in California discussing the issues surrounding the DH.108 and gathering information about American commercial airliner developments with several companies.

By the end of 1946, the design of the Comet had evolved to become more conventional with four jet engines buried in the wing roots and a return to a conventional tail. Cunningham left Heathrow on 20 November in a civilian Liberator, making the long flight across the Atlantic in three legs, stopping at Prestwick and Gander before reaching his first destination, the Canadian town of Dorval, and the aircraft company Canadair the following day. He flew only two aircraft while there—a Lockheed Constellation and the de Havilland Canada Chipmunk. The Constellation had a distinctive, elegant appearance with triple fins. It had been used during the war as a long-range troop transport, which meant that it could be easily adapted to the airliner configuration. Cunningham undertook concentrated crew training in the 'Connie' with a CPA Captain Pentland.

On Thursday, 12 December 1946, he arrived in Los Angeles at 6.40 a.m. and made his way to the Beverley Wilshire Hotel where accommodation had been arranged for him. With its Olympic-sized swimming pool and grand ballroom, it seems unlikely that the rather single-minded Cunningham would have been impressed or even made use of them. After the austerity of Britain, the luxury of America could not have failed to impress him, but he had little time to enjoy the luxury of his new surroundings. At 10 a.m., he left to visit the Northrop Corporation in Hawthorne to meet a team of Northrop's senior aerodynamicists and engineers. They spent an hour and a half discussing the loss of the DH.108 and shared experiences. Northrop was also researching the problems of high-speed flight related to 'flying wing' aircraft without tail units and had suffered their own problems. Cunningham kept pencil notes of his meetings:

Northrop lost one aircraft with fixed open slats that went on to its back and became completely stable in an inverted 'mush', the pilot abandoning aircraft, leaving it to crash to ground. Generally when stalled if a spin ensued it was inverted.

N.9.M new twin jet wing crashed on its first flight at a speed estimated between 250–400 mph, After perfectly normal take off and climb aircraft appeared to start a slow roll which continued into a steeper dive going straight into the ground. Cause of crash was not established but opinion of Northrop was probable mechanical jamming in controls.

N.9.M was a reference to one of Northrop's flying wing aircraft, first flown in 1942. Four were built with one crashing in a spin in May 1943, killing the pilot. The crash was attributed to control reversal, one of the problems associated with flight at transonic Mach numbers. The question mark suggests that Northrop had not been completely open as to which aircraft was being discussed, although Cunningham's notes go on to report problems with other 'flying wings', the XB-35 with contra-rotating propellers and the XB-49 powered by eight jet engines. At the time, such aircraft were being considered by the Americans as vehicles for delivering atomic bombs, but eventually, none entered service. In the case of the B-35, technical problems with the power plants and the propellers ended the development rather than aerodynamic problems.

Cunningham viewed mock-ups of two other aircraft relevant to his activities with de Havilland. The first was the X-4 Bantam, a tailless swept-wing experimental aircraft very similar to the DH.108 but about two-thirds the size. The second was a proposed night fighter: a development of the Lockheed P-80, originally capable of 0.81 Mach max. but later 0.86. This was achieved after going through some rough patches when the nose tended to drop at high speed. The later F-89 had two crew in tandem with an armament of 4 × 20-mm cannon and a nose-mounted radar. All fuel was carried in the fuselage. It had a very thin wing, with practically no sweep back, a conventional tail, and a rudder. The jet exhaust came out of the rear of the fuselage below the tail. Capability was supposed to be to climb to 35,000 feet and cruise for 1,000 miles at altitude, allowing for thirty minutes of combat, then 1,000 miles to return before let down and a further thirty minutes. In all, endurance was greater than fifty hours. Gross weight was approximately 38,000 lb with the radar scanner fitted above the gun barrels; it had an estimated top speed of 550 mph.

This was almost certainly a design in response to a USAAF specification for a replacement for the highly successful wartime Northrop P-61 Black Widow night fighter, of which Cunningham, with his interest and experience in night fighting, was likely to have been knowledgeable. During the war, the RAF had not had a purpose-built night fighter despite the success of the Beaufighter and Mosquito. The new fighter would go into service with the US Air Force and the Air National Guard as the F-89 Scorpion. First flown in August 1948, over 1,000 served with the American forces and it was only retired in 1969.

The following day saw a visit to the Lockheed Corporation in Burbank. The first hour was spent discussing the DH.108 in the context of Lockheed's P-80 Shooting Star, a single-seat interceptor already in USAAF service. The prototype was powered by a DH Goblin jet engine that also powered the DH.108. As before, the difficulties being investigated were in the approach to Mach 1, concentrating on shortcomings in the system to measure aircraft speed.

Lockheed also manufactured civil airliners, clearly of interest to Cunningham at that time. He inspected the Saturn, a small, high-wing, twin-engined aircraft intended for the feeder market, but which came to nothing because of the large number of surplus Douglas C-47 Skytrains being disposed of by the US government. Lockheed also made the Constellation, which he had been flying at Dorval a couple of weeks earlier. It is clear from his notes that he took an interest in improvements to the existing design, particularly to the braking and de-icing systems.

Yet another aeroplane, the Constitution, also attracted Cunningham's admiration. This aircraft had flown at the beginning of November so it was very new. It was enormous for its time. Some 156 feet long, it had a wingspan of 189 feet and the tail unit was 50 feet high. Initially conceived in 1942 as a joint venture by Lockheed, the US Navy, and Pan American Airways to produce a large transport aircraft, it was revolutionary for the time with a 'double-decker' fuselage configuration. Cunningham's notes were as follows:

> A remarkable machine … The cockpit has less for the pilot to worry about than any other big aircraft I have seen. All engine controls, apart from throttles, are handled by two flight engineers. Nose wheel steering is easier than the Constellation and Lockheed feels that the Constitution has the first really good power boost control system. This after seven years of development and over 4,000 aircraft built fitted with boost! The space on both floors is remarkable, at present mostly taken up by water ballast tanks which prove extremely satisfactory for any re-ballasting. All four engines are accessible in flight and main undercarriage retracts inwards to enable the fitting of take-off boost units at some later date. Gross weight 186,000 lb. Relatively little flying has been undertaken as yet but so far Lockheed is very happy with it.

The project came to nought for Lockheed. Only two Constitutions were built, both serving with the US Navy as long-range transports. However, Cunningham's notes reveal the pilot and the designer in him, particularly his comments about the cockpit.

For many years, accidents were often attributed solely to 'pilot error' if the pilot had either misinterpreted what was happening to the aeroplane or made a mistake in correcting the problem. However, more enlightened designers realised that the layout of the cockpit itself could be a factor and that it needed to be designed ergonomically to take account of the human factors. In modern aircraft which can induce large *g* forces on pilots, it might almost be impossible for a pilot to reach a switch or pull a lever that is some distance away from a hand, or indeed even see if he is about to 'grey' or 'red' out. Hence, modern cockpit design takes account of the ergonomics of pilot friendly design and the possibility of the pilot to make a mistake.

Cunningham therefore took a great interest in the cockpit and its layout, presumably for just such reasons. He also comments on the use of water for ballasting. The weight of an aircraft and its distribution affects the way it flies, and this changes while in flight as fuel is consumed. Thus, during flight testing, weight needs to be adjusted. In the early days, sandbags were used, or even a passing ground engineer who might be told to 'jump-in for a flip', but clearly water provided an easy method of changing weight and its distribution within the aircraft. After this, there was more discussion about sub-sonic flight and tail-less aircraft but perhaps most significant were glowing compliments for de Havilland and its work with the DH.108.

On Monday 16 December, it was the turn of the Douglas Aircraft Company in Santa Monica. As with the others, his first meeting discussed high-speed flight. In conjunction with the US Navy, Douglas was building a jet-powered research aircraft, the D-558-1 Skystreak. The layout was conventional with nose wheel, straight low aspect thin wing, and nose air intake.

He comments that Douglas did not consider ejection as a feasible means of escape at 'really high speed' so it was intended that the cockpit would be detached from the fuselage in the event of the aircraft breaking up. It also allowed the crew to operate in a 'shirt sleeve environment'. The project was to have had two phases—the jet-powered D-558-1 and the 558-2 powered by a single rocket. At the time of Cunningham's visit, it had not flown but it made its first flight in April 1947 from what is now Edwards Air Force Base. The aircraft briefly held a world speed record, but it was eventually overshadowed by the Bell rocket-powered experimental X-1, which subsequently exceeded Mach 1 flown by Major Chuck Yeager.

After this, it was back to commercial airliners and the Douglas DC-6, which would be in competition with the Lockheed Constellation seen by Cunningham the previous week. The DC-6 was a stretched derivative of the DC-4. Once again, he was particularly interested in the cockpit layout and the crew:

> Layout for domestic airlines using a crew of two. No Flight Engineer or Radio operator. All engine controls in front and thermal de-icing & cabin pressurisation controls are easily to hand for both pilots. It has nose-wheel steering and independent brakes and, unlike the DC-4, has been flown with both brakes operated together by only one pedal, and found to be entirely satisfactory. Pioneer automatic pilot fitted. The DC-6 is being fitted with weak points on the wing tips designed to break if excessive loads are applied in turbulent air.

The reduction of the number of crew members to two was presumably an attempt to reduce operating costs. Then another development was discussed, the DC-7. This was another transport with four engines and a further stretch of the DC-6.

Cunningham notes:

> Large slotted flaps and slotted ailerons fitted. Flaps can lower to 35 degrees and ailerons droop up to 20 degrees. Power boost is on the ailerons only. Elevator and Rudder controlled normally. The cockpit is fitted with 'bug-eyes' (overhead blisters in the canopy) giving pilots a better lateral view and behind.

Cunningham also comments that the pilots are too far apart and can only communicate by radio. He goes on: 'Built to a USAAF order, the military version had provision for a flight engineer, the layout is so complete that on long-distance flights, he can virtually be captain.'

As normally the pilot is the aircraft captain, Cunningham was, perhaps, unhappy with the concept of the flight engineer having such control. The DC-7 went on to be a very successful long-distance airliner and sold to BOAC, de Havilland's prime customer for the DH.106 Comet. On 23 December, he flew back to Heathrow aboard a Constellation as a crew member, leaving La Guardia airport in New York and stopping off at Shannon, Ireland.

The visits clearly gave Cunningham much food for thought—the sharing of information about high-speed flight and the developments of the American airliners that would be in competition with the Comet. The Comet, however, had one advantage over the aircraft he had seen—it was to be jet-powered. One apparently significant omission on his trip was the Boeing Airplane Company in Seattle, where the Boeing 707, a jetliner, was to become a serious competitor for the Comet.

Back in Britain, Cunningham, the company's chief test pilot (known as the head man), continued test flying the DH.108. Investigations continued into the specific causes of the high-speed disintegration of Geoffrey de Havilland's aeroplane discussed earlier. Cunningham concentrated on examining stalls, trimming, and landing approaches. In August, it was back to high-speed flight reaching Mach 0.83 at 35,000 feet. He completed over 150 flights in the DH.108.

For pilots flying aircraft in service (both military and civil), all of the characteristics of the aeroplane which they need to know intimately are established before they go into service and prospective pilots are taught how to fly within the aeroplane's defined limits. In the RAF, these characteristics are set out in documents (then known as pilot's notes) for each aircraft, now normally called the aircrew manual. Test pilots carry out research flights to discover the characteristics which will allow the routine operations in service (military and civil) to be carried out safely.

The DH.108 was specifically built to explore the unknown without previous experience with this type of experimental aircraft the pilots need to be individuals who, more than normal, remain calm under extreme conditions, and continue to process the information being presented to them. Many have died, and in the days before sophisticated telemetry, the pilot's observations, doing a commentary over the radio, often held the key to solving a problem. The need for trained test pilots was recognised in Britain with the establishment in 1943 of what would become the Empire Test Pilots' School, based at Farnborough and later Boscombe Down, where it continues to this day.

Another incident which illustrates the challenges involved a DH.110 prototype (later the Sea Vixen) in 1951. It had two Rolls-Royce Avon engines side by side in the fuselage. Each engine had an electrical generator providing power to the majority of systems. It had been assumed that with two generators, a full electrical failure was unlikely although a small battery was included to give about two minutes of emergency power. John had made the maiden flight of this prototype on 26 September 1951 and was testing the aircraft with Tony Richards as an observer, an account of their forced landing at Heathrow being given in John's own words in Chapter 8.

5

Comets

With John Derry now sharing DH.108 flight testing, Cunningham's involvement in that programme was reduced. He therefore turned his attention to other activities. On 31 August 1947, he gained his first FAI world record for a 100-km closed circuit in a Vampire at an average speed of 496.88 mph, although this record stood only for a matter of months. In March 1948, flying an experimental Ghost-engined Vampire F.1 TG/278 with increased wingspan, he took the world altitude record, climbing to a height of 59,446 feet, in recognition of which John was awarded the Britannia Trophy. The aircraft was used for high altitude development of the 5,000-lb thrust Ghost engine, four of which would power the Comet.

Two specially modified Lancastrians, a transport derivative of the Lancaster bomber, were used for endurance testing of the civil Ghost, with the outer two Merlins engines replaced by Ghosts. The Lancastrian was able to fly on the power of the two turbojets, and although unexciting, John spent many hours flying these aircraft to give practical experience of air intake shape and ram effect, fuel system operation, engine relight, jet pipe cooling, and many other features at relatively low speeds and an altitude restriction of 25,000 feet with the test aircraft.

To check crew visibility and rain dispersion, a Comet nose was fabricated and fitted on to the wooden front fuselage of a Horsa II troop-carrying glider. Flown by John, it was towed aloft by a Halifax and taken through precipitation before gliding back to Hatfield. With higher anticipated aerodynamic loads on the control surfaces, there was a need for power assistance, and this was accomplished on the DH.108 from May 1946, three years before the Comet flew.

A Comet nose wheel rig was created using a specially ballasted lorry chassis, stabilised by out-rigged Mosquito main wheels, but at least John did not have to fly such a contraption. All these tests were to ensure the Comet technical risk was at a minimum. These were complementary to a full-scale control systems rig set up in the factory and operated continuously for over three years, to determine the practical endurances of the component parts, to assess and improve failure rates and provide for spares and overhaul.

A rig was built in the Experimental Department to test the systems operation and extensive structural testing was undertaken of components, sub-assemblies and major assemblies, all known established structural criteria being achieved with adequate safety margins.

Test pilots are a special breed of men, and occasionally women, who take their flying tasks seriously and highly professionally. They have to fly very precisely, observe and record. They work in an engineering and scientific environment, which removes any flamboyant tendencies. At the same time, test pilots are also expected to demonstrate their charges, where they perform as high-powered salesman demonstrating all the advantages of the aircraft type within the restricted boundaries of a show airfield, from high-performance jet combat aircraft to a single-engined basic trainer.

With the increasing demand for production, de Havilland acquired the large Government factory at Broughton with its adjacent RAF airfield at Hawarden, near Chester. Vickers Armstrong had used the factory for the mass production of Wellington and Lancaster bombers during the Second World War, and the front door was formed in the logo of VA. The overall factory was larger than Hatfield, and with its network of overhead cranes, capable of lifting entire aircraft, it was the most modern in Europe. John had the responsibility for the test flying at this site, as well as the others in use by the de Havilland companies.

The Broughton factory was responsible for the construction of Vampires and Venoms for the RAF and export, together with the Dove light transport and later the larger four-engined Heron. While the prototypes were designed and developed at Hatfield, with sometimes initial production, the major production effort was at Broughton. There were still some of the last Mosquitos being built at Broughton, as well as Hornets and Sea Hornets for the RAF and FAA. In addition, after starting assembly at Hatfield, de Havilland Canada's first original design, the Chipmunk, was produced at Broughton, a total of 1,000 being built in the UK for the RAF and export, in many cases replacing the venerable Tiger Moth. Pat Fillingham, who had flown more Mosquitos than any other pilot while he was testing the aircraft coming off the production lines in Britain, Canada and Australia, was the project pilot for the Chipmunk.

John, with his wartime experience as the commanding officer of 604 and 85 Squadrons, had developed his gift for selecting pilots. In 1948, he brought in Norwegian pilot Peter 'Per' Bugge as a development test pilot to share the Comet flight testing. Peter had escaped from occupied Norway by boat, almost missing the north of Scotland; he was one of three Norwegians who had joined 604 Squadron in the winter of 1941–42 to train as night fighter pilots. Peter Bugge was a quiet unassuming person, who was always pleasant and courteous, and had shared a second tour with John on 85 Squadron, serving with distinction. On his return to Norway after the war, he became a civil airline pilot, initially flying twin-engined Lodestars, followed by four engine DC-4s from Stockholm to Leuchars in Scotland. John also hired Peter Bois, another wartime colleague, who was flying with SAS. Thus, both Peters had airline experience, including four engine airliners, ideal for the planned Comet development. Peter Bugge was later to become

John's deputy, while Pat Fillingham was chief production test pilot.

Although keen, John never got married. He was about to become engaged just before being sent to Burma at the end of the war, but on his return, he found that his fiancée-to-be had married a colleague in 11 Group. Later in 1947–48, John met another young lady, but unfortunately their plans fell through, although they continued to meet occasionally. When asked in more recent years why he had never married, his answer was that when he had been asked the same question by an airline president in South America, he said, 'she is out there on the airport apron—the Comet'. John's work ethic was that if flying demanded it, he would fly seven days a week to ensure development would not be delayed, Saturdays and Sundays included. Meanwhile, he enjoyed the simple things of life including his garden, often bringing in produce to work, and the countryside with its wildlife.

With such a new concept as a jet airliner, the design and production teams had many challenges to overcome. Every component had to be tested, not just individually, but also in sub-assemblies and major assemblies. Weight was critical as the initial Comet 1s would be powered by four Ghost engines, while preparing for the ultimate Comet 2 and 3 to be powered by higher thrust and more efficient Rolls-Royce axial flow turbo-jet Avons. The Avon engines were delayed in gaining civil certification, although they were gaining hours flying in military aircraft. For civil applications in the Comet, the Ghost engine had to be 80 per cent redesigned from its military origins, with a central air intake, becoming the world's first civil turbo-jet engine.

John, as well as being chief test pilot, was an essential member of the design team, advising on aerodynamics, handling, flight-deck layout (including instrumentation and controls), and low-speed handling for approach and landing at existing worldwide airports. Clear, precise controllability was essential with effective balanced handling, without the benefit of modern-day simulators. The aircraft had to be able to take off from existing runways with an economic payload and fly passengers in comfort over regular stage lengths, saving them time in competition with existing propeller-driven airliners. The Comet could fly above the weather, where turbulence was much reduced, and the cabin environment had to be comfortable for passengers of all ages and health. The Comet was in effect a major step in aviation, just as Concorde was two decades later, but without the massive cost overruns and delays experienced by the Anglo-French supersonic airliner. The Comet was to be an economic airliner to build and operate, not a loss leader. While the design and construction were underway, the company kept a high level of commercial security, and the chief designer, R. E. Bishop, who had led the Mosquito design, kept a purposefully inaccurate model of a jet airliner project in his office to mislead visitors.

The first prototype Comet was hand-built in the Experimental Department using production tooling and was a traditional aluminium structure with slightly swept-back wings and a traditional tail with a single fin and rudder. Another pioneering process used was Redux bonding of the aluminium skins which had been developed from the adhesives used in the Mosquito, through wood to metal bonding with the composite Hornet and then for the first time metal to metal bonding in the Dove. Bonding saved weight, so essential in early jet airliners, by avoiding drilling the skins to fasten with rivets or bolts, which inherently weaken the structure.

John's and the other test pilot offices were just outside the experimental hangar, where he could visit to advise on any aspect involved with flying and operating the aircraft. The de Havilland design and production teams worked very closely together to ensure that what was being designed could be built and subsequently safely flown.

The Comet prototype was pulled out backwards from the experimental hangar on 2 April 1949, with a pair of Ghosts fitted in the port wing root. Once the other two engines were installed, engine runs started of the polished aluminium aircraft, checking their performance and systems operation. Following a compass swing to check any compass errors, the prototype was close to flight. On Sunday, 27 July 1949, the media were invited to see the Comet for the first time, and John and his crew were able to demonstrate some runs down the runway with short hops, before the press departed.

Much to his surprise, the aircraft was declared ready later in the afternoon, and he decided to make the maiden flight with John Wilson as second pilot, Frank Reynolds as flight engineer, Harry Walters as electrician, and Tony Fairbrother as flight test observer. John Wilson had only recently joined the company and was therefore the most junior pilot, but if there had been a disaster, John Cunningham did not want to lose another experienced pilot. It was a long time before the press forgave de Havilland for not making the first flight public, but no initial flight can be made to a timetable.

Both Cunningham's logbook and his test report record the duration of the flight as thirty-five minutes, although it was preceded by another 'short hop with full flap'. After the final hop, he took off at 6.17 p.m. and climbed towards a clear patch of sky. Reaching 10,000 feet, he checked handling at low and medium speeds before lowering the undercarriage and flaps to check the landing configuration, leaving plenty of altitude to recover from any unexpected problems. Satisfied with this, he then brought the Comet back to the airfield and made a low pass for the benefit of company employees before making an uneventful landing, and a welcome from the team who had built the aircraft. John had made the first flight on his thirty-second birthday, and when he briefed Sir Geoffrey de Havilland the next day, the founder admitted they both shared a birthday.

The flight was not without its problems, but they were relatively trivial, possibly the most significant being a shudder in the airframe caused by the mechanism designed to bring the control surfaces back to a neutral position after being moved to change the attitude of the aeroplane. Overall, it was a good start, as extracts from the test record show:

The aircraft came off the ground in about 500 yards and on reaching about 50 feet Height. I selected u/c up. As the speed was increasing rather quickly I throttled down to about 9,500 to 9,750 r.p.m. and 135k. About this moment the windscreen wiper blade on the starboard side started to rotate. A position was found where it could be parked out of sight for the remainder of the flight. During the climb at 200 kts I found all controls very powerful and highly geared. The spring centring on all controls produced a pronounced jerk throughout the machine on releasing the control after slight displacement. Wheels were next selected down when it was noticed that no lights were showing although the mechanical indicators showed 'locked down'. On replacing the circuit breakers I noticed there was no green light for the port main wheel, although the mechanical indicator shows 'Down'. A gradual descent was made back to the airfield, during which it was extremely hard to lose speed. After a low flypast at 150-160 kts down the runway, a wide circuit was made, and the final approach to land was completed at 100 kts. The landing and touchdown were perfectly straightforward, and very little braking was required owing to a fairly strong wind.

The next day, it was back to more routine work with a routine flight in the DH.108 and a check flight in a Vampire. On Thursday 4 August, Cunningham began a concentrated series of test flights in the Comet starting with three to test trim, stalls, and aileron drop. The next day, it was stalls and rates of descent. Over the following days and weeks, the testing continued but not exclusively by Cunningham. The new aeroplane achieved much, flying from Edinburgh to Brighton in forty-two minutes, and the Shetland Islands to Hatfield in sixty minutes. On 25 October 1949, Cunningham took the Comet from London to Libya and back in twelve hours, on its first overseas flight.

John's daily life was demanding, an example being the preparation for the first flight overseas—he flew the Comet prototype to Heathrow on two consecutive days, carrying out a series of night landings and GCA approaches in mixed October weather, to familiarise himself with the airport and its control procedures, towards the end operating in very poor visibility. On 24 October, the day following these flights, John and his crew departed Hatfield at about 9.30 p.m., arriving at a less busy Heathrow about ten minutes later.

The crew retired to bed and were up again at 4 a.m., checking the weather and being briefed on navigational and radio operations. At around 6 a.m., John, Peter Bugge (first officer), Brackstone-Brown (flight engineer), and Blackett (navigator and radio operator) climbed the steps of the aircraft; they took off in darkness and light rain at 6.33 a.m. Climbing through cloud at 31,000 feet to 35,000 feet, they arrived at Castle Benito, Tripoli, three hours and twenty-three minutes after take-off. After a welcome and late breakfast, they returned to London for lunch, having been to Africa and back in half a day.

In March 1950, John gained four inter-capital records, out and back to Rome and Copenhagen. Everywhere the Comet flew, it established new rapid times. Hatfield to Rome was flown on 16 March in a time of two hours, two minutes, and fifty-two seconds, achieving an overall speed of 447.246 mph. The return took nearly two more minutes, reducing the average speed to 442.326 mph, the record being based on the equivalent city centre times. On 21 March, Hatfield to Copenhagen was flown in one hour, eighteen minutes, and 36.5 seconds, and return in one hour, twenty-four minutes, and fifty-two seconds, giving average speeds of 453.98 mph and 420.36 mph respectively.

A month later, John took the prototype on tropical trials in Africa to measure performance in hot and high conditions. This entailed leading a team of up to twenty people with all the equipment for measuring the results. The outbound flight from Hatfield to Cairo on 24 April covering 2,182 miles in five hours and nine minutes, averaging 426.63 mph. The next day, John took the Comet 2,195 miles to Nairobi in five hours and fifteen minutes, at an average speed of around 420 mph. The aircraft was loaded with the equivalent of thirty-four passengers and baggage from the restricted

Hatfield runway. The most demanding part of the performance testing was from Nairobi, where the altitude was 5,370 feet above sea level in temperatures of 34 degrees C or 93 degrees F. For higher temperatures at close to sea level, Khartoum was used, with the team returning to Hatfield on 11 May.

Among later tests was an assisted take-off from Hatfield with a pair of Sprite rocket engines between G-ALVG Ghost jet pipes in May 1951, to improve performance when taking off with heavy loads from hot and high airfields, although it was not adopted in practice. To extend range, in-flight refuelling was considered and John flew a Meteor IV to link up with a tanker Lancaster, followed by flying G-ALVG fitted with a refuelling probe. Connecting the probe into the hose on a number of occasions was not considered practical for airlines.

The first Comet prototype—G-ALVG—had a large single main wheel undercarriage, but a four-wheel bogie main undercarriage was tested on the prototype, although it could not be retracted. John took the second prototype—G-ALZK—on its maiden flight on 27 July 1950, exactly a year after the initial maiden flight. In September 1950, John demonstrated G-ALVG at the SBAC show at Farnborough in BOAC colours as its introduction to the public.

The first production Comet 1 G-ALYP was flown by John on 9 January 1951 to join the flight development programme, to confirm the production standard. By this time, the two prototypes had flown 525 hours, the first aircraft being used for aerodynamics testing and performance measurement. The second prototype was used for systems development, and on completion was delivered to BOAC on 2 April 1951 for route proving this new concept in air transport. Following a crew training programme led by John, G-ALZK was used for the exploration of jet airliner operation techniques in preparation for delivery of the first service aircraft later in the year. Among the areas studied were air traffic control effects, high altitude meteorological studies over the BOAC global route structure, the measurement of cruise economy and performance, and checking radio and navigation aids, the aircraft having a flight deck crew of two pilots, a flight engineer, and navigator. The programme was compiled and monitored in co-operation with the airworthiness authorities, who were creating new standards of safe operation.

During the first eight weeks with BOAC, G-ALZK flew 147 hours, initially around Britain for performance measurements, but then extending on the route structure to Cairo, Calcutta, and further afield. No passengers were carried on these operations, as the cabin was not furnished. As overseas proving flights developed, seats were fitted in the cabin to accommodate VIPs who helped to promote the Comet at overseas destinations where it created much interest. One of the flights in the series was London to Johannesburg on 17–18 July 1951, taking an elapsed time of seventeen hours and thirty-three minutes via Cairo and Entebbe, covering 6,212 miles, of which fifteen hours and nine minutes were flying time. This operation was a rehearsal for the joint BOAC/SAA 'Springbok Service', and in two years of testing, four Comets had flown more than 1,000 hours, with deliveries to BOAC imminent.

The fourth Comet made its first flight on 28 July 1951, almost two years to the day of the original maiden flight. On 19 October 1951, G-ALZK returned to Heathrow, having completed twelve overseas tours in six months, coving 91,000 miles in 460 hours, and made ninety-one landings at thirty-one overseas airports. In addition to gathering data on long-range cruise performance in all climates, traffic patterns were investigated at major airports, including alternative approach procedures at Heathrow. Technical delays were minimal, mainly cured by the normal provision of spares established around the route network.

As a result of the total flight development programme led by John, it was shown the Comet, even in its early developed form, could fit into the route patterns with no difficulty and was well suited to airport approach patterns without penalty. Both air and ground crew found the Comet easy to operate, with good serviceability and favourable handling. The fast high-altitude smooth over the weather flying was expected to make the Comet popular with passengers.

Following all the testing, the Comet was awarded the world's first jet air transport Certificate of Airworthiness (C of A) on 22 January 1952 by the Ministry of Civil Aviation, the candidate aircraft being the fifth Comet G-ALYS. With the C of A achieved, deliveries of Comet 1s began to Heathrow, the first to arrive being G-ALYS on 4 February 1952, handed over six months ahead of contract date by John to Captain A. M. Majendie, BOAC Comet fleet manager, for crew training and formal route proving led by John.

The arrival of G-ALYU and G-ALYP on 6 and 13 March allowed preparations for the world's first commercial jet passenger service on 2 May 1952, leaving Heathrow for Johannesburg commanded by Captain Majendie, carrying thirty passengers. Among those waving off the inaugural flight were Sir Geoffrey de Havilland and John Cunningham. It was a proud moment for the company and for Britain.

With the Comet becoming established in BOAC passenger service, John flew the recently widowed HRH Queen Elizabeth the queen mother, Princess Margaret, and Lord and Lady Salisbury on an afternoon jet airliner tour of Europe. Hosted by Sir Geoffrey and Lady de Havilland, John flew for four hours on a tour around France, Switzerland, Northern Italy, and across the Pyrenees. John invited the queen mother to sit in the captain's seat and take the controls, while Peter Bugge was in the right-hand seat. Her majesty was delighted with her experience and wanted to know if she had flown faster than the pilots of 600 Squadron Meteors, of which she was honorary air commodore. The duke of Edinburgh had been given a Comet ride in March 1952, and visibility was bad on approaching Hatfield, with the duke sitting on the 'jump seat' between the two pilots. John used his knowledge of local landmarks, bringing the aircraft into line with the approach lights for finals.

Meanwhile, on 16 February 1952, John had made the first flight of the development Comet 2 G-ALYT, an adaptation of a Series 1 from the BOAC order, with power coming from four 6,500-lb thrust Rolls-Royce Avon engines. This allowed payload to be increased from thirty-six passengers in Comet 1s to up to forty-four passengers, and greater fuel capacity giving increased range. BOAC ordered twelve of this version.

In September 1952, John lost two colleagues when John Derry and Tony Richards were demonstrating the DH.110 prototype WG236 at the Farnborough Show on 6 September. As John Derry pulled up in front of the crowd after breaking the sound barrier, there was a structural failure in the wings, with the aircraft breaking up at high speed. As the aircraft disintegrated, one of the Avon engines continued towards the crowd, hitting the ground, killing twenty-nine spectators and injuring sixty seriously. Derry had recently written in *The Times Survey of British Aviation* that it was through hard schools of research and development, and later operational flying, that new territories of speed can be made safe and comfortable for all. The work is done by a team, and of that team, the test pilot can be likened to a doctor who must diagnose the patient's malady by careful examination of the systems, through understanding and experience.

The investigation found that there was torsional failure of the wing during a combination of high acceleration and rate of roll, causing the leading-edge wing skins to peel back. The grounded second prototype (WG240) was modified by reinforcing the wing structure with skin doubler plates, and the tail outline revised. John Cunningham recommenced flight testing the DH.110 in the spring of 1953, when it became the first British aircraft with an all-moving tailplane.

John concentrated on flying the Comet 2 G-ALYT prototype to determine performance with the Avon engines, including the fitting of a water spray rig forward of the inboard starboard engine to check for the effects of icing. Meanwhile, the factory was turning out production Comet 1As for export, involving production flight testing, crew training, and customer acceptance flight, often followed by delivery. Crew training was 'free' as part of the contract, and a number of operators sent not only their most senior captains, but also a number of junior pilots for John's team to train on the operation of the Comet.

The first Comet 1A for UAT (F-BGSA) was the first overseas delivery on 11 December 1952 to Le Bourget, ready for route proving and crew training flights on their West African routes, with regular services commencing in February 1953. The two RCAF Comet 1As were used for VIP transport and simulated high-speed jet bomber penetration to test the country's defences. Comet 1A VC5301 was the first jet transport to cross the North Atlantic when it was delivered to 412 Squadron on 29 May 1953. Air France took delivery of their first Comet 1A F-BGNX on 12 June 1953, with services inaugurated from Paris to Beirut on 12 June 1953. The twenty-second and last Series 1A F-BGNZ was delivered to Air France on 22 July 1953, leaving the factory busy with the build-up of Comet 2 production.

Comets began to settle down to regular operations with BOAC, expanding from London to Colombo on 11 August with stops at Rome, Beirut, Bahrain, Karachi and Bombay—now Mumbai, followed by service extension to Singapore on 14 October and Tokyo in early 1953, with the last of nine Comets (G-ALYZ) delivered on 30 September. It was lost in a non-fatal take-off accident at Rome on 26 October 1952, when the crew over-rotated during take-off, resulting in the wing becoming stalled and an overrun beyond the end of the runway. John had warned of this phenomenon during crew training, but had not been heeded. The problem was caused by the lack of propeller wash over the wings giving lift during the take-off run, and the cure was to ensure that even with the tail skid running along the ground, the aircraft would still be able to safely take off—a technique common to all jet airliners. John carried out a series of tests at Hatfield, roaring down the runway pulling the nose higher and higher to reproduce the conditions of the Rome accident, to establish cause and remedy.

Export Comets to an improved specification designated Series 1A were coming out of the factory, the first (CF-CUM) flying on 11 August 1952. This was the first of two destined for Canadian Pacific Airways (CPA), used for performance measurements of the improved all-up weight (auw). The second for CPA (CF-CUN) was destroyed on take-off from Karachi on 2 March 1953, caused by over-rotating and stalling the wing.

It was commanded by Captain Charles Pentland, who had flown with John when he was experiencing the Constellation and had been trained by John on the Comet, who demonstrated what would happen if the nose was pulled too far back on take-off. Captain Pentland had said, 'Holy Jeez, how on Earth did the chap do that?' when referring to the Rome accident. Captain Pentland was attempting to achieve a record time for England to Australia and started his first night take-off from Karachi at maximum weight for a non-stop flight to Rangoon with a ground haze obscuring the horizon. Despite John's instructions on the revised take-off technique, Pentland allowed the nose to lift prematurely on the take-off run. Realising what was happening, he lowered the nose and belatedly became airborne. However, it was too late; the Comet hit a drainage culvert and exploded in flames fed by the full load of fuel.

John briefed Bishop, who made a pencil drawing of a droop wing leading edge, which was made within twenty-four hours and incorporated on all Comets, allowing safe take-off with the tail on the ground, but not recommended operationally due to skin damage to the fuselage. As a result, CPA did not take the surviving Series 1A, which went to BOAC as G-ANAV.

On 20 October 1952, a major sales breakthrough was made in the highly competitive American market with an order from PanAm for three Comet 3s.

John made the maiden flight of the first Comet 2 G-AMXA for BOAC on 27 August 1953, one of the modifications incorporated being an improved wing section giving better take-off performance, improved slow flying characteristics, reduced landing speed, and made it impossible to stall the wing during the take-off run. The Avon was originally expected to develop 6,500 lb thrust. The development programme allowed an increase to 7,150 lb thrust, improving take-off performance, with the overhaul life to reach 1,000 hours once in regular commercial service. The Comet 2 had a 15,000-lb increase in AUW over the Comet 1 and was able to carry a payload of 13,450 lb. A typical long-range operation was the 2,116 miles from Caracas to New York in a time of five hours and nineteen minutes, cruising between 480 and 500 mph.

At 2 p.m. GMT on 2 May 1953, BOAC completed their first year of commercial jet airliner operations, but this significant achievement was marred two hours before by the loss of Comet 1 G-ALYV after take-off from Calcutta on its way to London. While climbing away at around 10,000 feet, the aircraft entered a violent storm with cumulonimbus thunder clouds, heavy turbulence and lightning. When almost through to cruising altitude, the Comet went out of control into a high-speed dive, disintegrating as it fell to the ground as a result of the high structural loads, killing all thirty-seven passengers and six crew. No aircraft could be expected to survive in such turbulent conditions, and therefore the Comet was not displaying any inherent structural weakness, but it did result in the eventual development of radar to avoid violent weather.

Then news came in of the loss of a BOAC Comet 1 in mysterious circumstances. The first production aircraft (G-ALYP) came down in the sea off Elba after take-off from Rome on Sunday 10 January 1954. The aircraft *en route* from Singapore to London, with the loss of all twenty-nine passengers and six crew. On the following day, BOAC in conjunction with the Air Registration Board (ARB) and de Havilland temporarily suspended Comet passenger operations to allow detailed inspections of the aircraft. Some sixty precautionary modifications were made to the remaining aircraft in the fleet, covering all suspected causes of the disaster, allowing the ARB to permit services to be resumed on 23 March.

Meanwhile, Comet 2 development continued with John leading a flight development team in G-AMXA on tropical trials at Khartoum and Johannesburg from 22 January to 6 February 1954, gaining the London to Khartoum record of 481 mph in an elapsed time of six hours, twenty-four minutes, and nineteen seconds over a distance of 3,080 miles. Following analysis of the results, the Comet 2 had not only achieved its performance targets, but was significantly better than expected.

The Comet had left Hatfield at its full AUW of 120,000 lb, including a full fuel load of 6,920 gallons and a payload of 10,500 lb, which represented forty-four passengers and their baggage. On landing at Khartoum, the base for high ambient temperature trials, the Comet had sufficient fuel for a 400-mile diversion with a thirty-minute hold for landing. During the hot and high trials at Jan Smuts Airport for Johannesburg at an elevation of 5,559 feet above sea level, the Comet performed faultlessly throughout.

BOAC signed a contract for five of the stretched Comet 3s on 1 February 1954, the airliner being years ahead of any competition. The increased speeds gave greater utilisation, helping to bring down the cost of air travel to the public. Flying high above the weather, Comets achieved journey times half of that expected with piston-engined airliners, with much greater comfort.

Then disaster struck again. BOAC Comet 1 G-ALYY was lost off Stromboli on 8 April 1954. Fourteen passengers and seven crew were killed, with the wreckage falling in a deep part of the Mediterranean Sea near Naples, mostly beyond recovery. All passenger-carrying Comets were grounded and the C of A withdrawn on 12 April, pending a full investigation into the cause. Work had already been started by the Royal Navy on the challenging recovery of 'Yoke Peter' from the sea bed near Elba.

The widely scattered wreckage lay at depths of between 450 and 600 feet, and due to the technology available at the time, divers and equipment were able to go down only 200 feet. The problem was also locating the wreckage, but photos of a rescue craft from an aircraft flying overhead helped to pinpoint the main area to search. A Malta-based salvage vessel pioneered the use of underwater television to detect possible components, the first piece of wreckage being located on 10 February. The first piece to be raised was the rear cabin including the pressure dome. Overall, some 75 per cent of the wreckage was recovered, including the cockpit and wing centre-section containing all four Ghost engines. There were no flight data or cockpit voice recorders carried at this time.

Above left: John flying Moth Minor G-AFRD over Dunstable Downs for sales brochure.

Above right: Burning wreckage of Moth Minor G-AFRD near Wheathamstead on 11 April 1939.

Right: John usually carried his camera and took a photo of his parachute spread out on the ground.

Left: Wartime charcoal portrait of John, 17 November 1941.

Below: Jimmy Rawnsley and John by a Mosquito night fighter.

Above: John (centre) relaxing with a beer during the Second World War.

Right: A young Wg Cdr John Cunningham, commanding officer (CO) of 604 Squadron, at Middle Wallop.

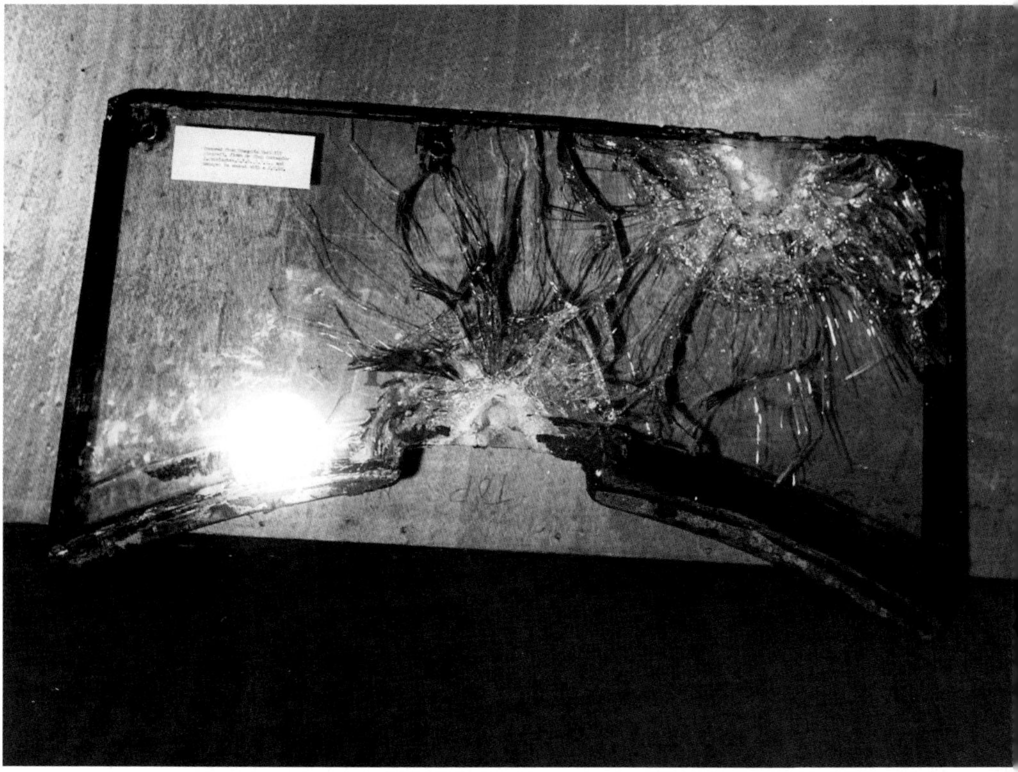

Above: The damaged laminated Mosquito windscreen after being hit by gunfire from a Luftwaffe He 111.

Left: Wg Cdr John Cunningham, CO of 85 Squadron at Hunsdon.

Above and below: Wg Cdr John Cunningham at Hunsdon when 85 Squadron was presented with its squadron crest.

Left: Grp Capt. John Cunningham by a Mosquito.

Below: Royal Swedish Air Force Vampire F.1s lined up at Hatfield ready for delivery with underwing ferry fuel tanks.

Royal Swedish Air Force Vampire FB.6.

Swiss Vampire F.1 at Hatfield being pushed out with John's help on the wing tip wearing a trilby hat, ready for delivery with long-range ferry tanks under the wings.

First pair of Swiss Vampire F.1 evaluation batch being prepared for departure, with John flying one.

When John delivered Vampires to Switzerland, he often enjoyed winter sports and strapped his skis to the tail booms.

The Ghost test-bed Lancastrian VM703 was first flown by John on 24 July 1947 and could fly on jet power alone with the Merlins stopped.

Six-engined Lancastrian take-off from Hatfield including a pair of Sprite rocket boosters proposed for Comet hot and high weight take-offs.

Left: John climbing aboard the high-altitude Ghost-powered Vampire TG/278.

Below: High-altitude Ghost-powered Vampire with increased wingspan and pressure cabin in which John achieved an altitude record height of 59,446 feet on 23 March 1948.

John taxying in a Hatfield following achieving his altitude record.

DH.108 VW120 used for high-speed research and exceeded the speed of sound on 9 September 1948, the first time outside the USA and in an aircraft that took off and returned to the airfield under its own power.

DH.110 WG240 was demonstrated at the Farnborough Air Show in September 1953 by John Cunningham, having been strengthened following the loss if the first prototype the previous year. John had made the maiden flight of DH.110 WG236 on 26 September 1951, just missing the Farnborough Show that year.

Horsa II TL348 had its original swing nose replaced by a mock-up of the Comet nose on the same diameter fuselage to check levels of crew visibility.

John flew Horsa II TL348 towed behind a Halifax bomber looking for rain squalls to check the performance of the windscreen wipers.

John made the maiden flight of the Comet jet airliner from Hatfield on 27 July 1949.

Left: John being introduced to the queen mother with Sir Geoffrey de Havilland. Facing the camera in the centre is Frank Halford, DH Ghost engine designer; Ronald Bishop, Comet designer; and HRH Princess Margaret.

Below: Classic lines of Comet prototype G-ALVG in initial BOAC markings.

Comet 1 flight deck with captain in the left-hand seat, first officer in the right-hand seat, navigator behind the captain, and flight engineer behind the first officer.

Comet 1 prototype G-ALVG in full BOAC markings demonstrated at Farnborough by John Cunningham in September 1950.

Comet prototype G-ALVG flew tropical trails at Khartoum.

Comet prototype G-ALVG with take-off from Hatfield boosted by a pair of Sprite rocket engines.

Second prototype Comet 1 G-ALZK was first flown by John on 27 July 1950, one year after the first.

Sir Geoffrey de Havilland, HRH Princess Margaret, and John on Comet 1 flight deck.

John with DH.51 *Miss Kenya* in Nairobi during Comet tropical trials. This aircraft is now preserved at the Shuttleworth Trust.

Left: The Rolls-Royce Avon-powered Comet 2 prototype G-ALYT, which was first flown by John on 16 February 1952.

Below: Peter Bugge, deputy chief test pilot, and John in front of Comet 4.

John with HRH the duke of Edinburgh on Comet 1 flight deck.

John and Peter Bugge on Comet 4 flight deck. Peter was from Norway originally and flew with John in the Second World War.

Above: First Comet 2 G-AMXA, first flown by John on 27 August 1953, but never delivered to BOAC.

Left: John in a rare pose at his desk.

Above: Comet 3 G-ANLO was first flown by John on 19 July 1954 and was used for aerodynamic development of the Comet 4.

Right: Comet 3 G-ANLO in Hawaii during the first round the world flight by a jet airliner in December 1955. In recognition of this achievement, John was awarded the Harman Trophy by the president of the USA.

Peter Bugge and John.

Comet 3B XP915 ex G-ANLO, was operated by the Blind Landing Experimental Unit (BLEU) at RAE Bedford for Trident Autoland development.

Above: Comet 4 G-APDA, the first of nineteen for BOAC, was flown for the first time from Hatfield by John on 27 April 1958.

Right: John being interviewed by the press on his return from the first flight of Comet 4 G-APDA.

Comet 4 G-APDA at Rio de Janiero, Brazil, during a sales demonstration tour of South America.

The first Comet 4 export customer was Aerolineas Argentinas, who ordered an initial batch of three aircraft.

Comet 3B G-ANLO in front of the Hatfield control tower. John's office was just above the title 'European' on the aircraft fuselage.

King Saud's VIP Comet 4C SA-R-7, the world's first airliner business jet, was lost in the Alps on 20 March 1963.

Left: John wearing the uniform of a United Arab Airlines captain with the airline chief pilot, Captain Shams. In addition to test flying, John also undertook customer airline pilot crew training.

Below: Five Comet C.4s were operated by 216 Squadron from RAF Lyneham on global communications.

The Comet 4 was the basis of the RAF Nimrod XV147 maritime reconnaissance aircraft powered by Rolls-Royce Spey turbofans.

Comet 2R with two R-R Avon RA 29 engines in the outboard positions was used by BOAC for engine development before being allocated to Smiths Industries for Trident Autoland development.

A rare occasion when all four Dove Mk 8s from the HSA communications fleet were at Hatfield together.

John made the maiden flight of the Trident 1 G-ARPA from Hatfield on 9 January 1962.

Following the first flight of the Trident 1, the crew were congratulated by the employees. From the bottom of the steps were John, Peter Bugge, Brax, Tony Fairbrother (flight development), John Marshall (instrument laboratory), and John Johnston (flight development).

Trident 1 G-ARPB was used for Autoland development before delivery to BEA.

Six Trident 1s of the flight development fleet together on the Hatfield flight test apron on the return of G-ARPE from a Middle East sales tour.

Trident 1 G-ARPY on pressure test before its first production test flight when it crashed in a deep stall on 3 June 1966, killing the crew.

Wreckage of BEA Trident 1 G-ARPI in the accident investigation hangar at Farnborough which crashed in a deep stall after take-off from Heathrow on 18 June 1972, killing all on board.

Above: John with Colonel Yuri Gagarin, the Russian space cosmonaut who made the first human orbit of the earth in space on 12 April 1961.

Below left: John with the author monitoring progress with the annual Hatfield flying open day held on the first Saturday in July.

Below right: John by Trident 1 G-ARPB at Hatfield.

Export Trident 1E G-ASWU at Hatfield for development flying before delivery to Kuwait Airways.

Pakistan International Trident 1E AP-ATL, the first of four for the airline and later sold to CAAC of China.

John made the first flight of Trident Two for BEA from Hatfield on 27 July 1967, once again on his birthday.

Trident 2 G-AVFA at Hatfield fitted with a long nose probe for flight development.

Hubert Broad, de Havilland test pilot of the 1920s and '30s; Rod banks, general manager at Hatfield; and John at one of the annual Hatfield flying open days.

John and the flight test team making a presentation to Ernie Pankhurst on his retirement. Ernie was the duty marshal of the visiting aircraft to Hatfield aerodrome.

John with CAAC Trident 2 G-BBWD at Hatfield.

CAAC of China Trident 2 G-AZFY/250.

CAAC Trident Super Three G-BAJL, one of two of this high-density version delivered to China, making its first flight by John on 9 July 1975.

John at Hatfield annual flying display with Chrisair Dragon, including Jimmy Phillips, project pilot for Trident Autoland; Pat Fillingham on steps, chief production test pilot during the Second World War; Hubert Broad; and Ron Clear, Trident development test pilot.

Right: Reggie Moon being congratulated by John on his retirement as communications pilot at Hatfield and ex-CFI at Panshanger.

Below: Gathering of flight test personnel in front of Dove 8 G-AREA on the occasion of Pat Fillingham's retirement (centre) with John making the presentation.

Above left: John and Peter Owen, Trident design at the formal company celebration of John's retirement.

Above right: John flew in Comet 4C XS235 *Canopus* from Boscombe Down on 20 July 1996, close to the forty-seventh anniversary of the Comet's first flight on 27 July 1949.

The last time John was at the controls of an aircraft in Comet 4C XS235 *Canopus* on 20 July 1996.

Above left: Formal portrait of Group Captain John Cunningham with DSO and DFC.

Above right: John checking his flying log book during the interview.

Right: Formal portrait of John wearing his 85 Squadron tie.

John and Peter Bugge with Comet 3 in 1956.

Frank Hearle, unknown, John, and Sir Geoffrey de Havilland in front of high-altitude Ghost Vampire after gaining the height record.

Above left: Comet 1's first flight crew being congratulated on 27 July 1949 after returning to the Experimental Department.

Above right: John, Sir Geoffrey de Havilland, Peter Bugge, and Sir Miles Thomas (chairman of BOAC).

Below: John on the steps of Comet 3 G-ANLO during the around the world flight.

Peter Bugge, John, BOAC Captain Peter Cane, and Quantas Captain Ralfe during the Comet 3's around the world flight.

Hatfield Open Day by Hornet Moth G-ADND with Frank Reynolds, Hubert Broad, John, Bob Hardingham (ARB), and Reggie Moon.

Mosquito prototype W4050 was flown for the first time by Geoffrey de Havilland Jnr from Hatfield on 25 November 1940.

John by Mosquito NF.II prototype.

Geoffrey de Havilland Jnr flying DH.108 TG306, which crashed into Egypt Bay in the Thames Estuary on 27 September 1946 during a high-speed flight. The aircraft broke up and the pilot was killed.

Moth Minor E.6.

Mosquito NF.XV DZ366 on 22 May 1943.

DH.108 TG/283 at Hatfield on 17 March 1948.

DH.108 VW120, used for high-speed research.

Left: John Derry.

Below: Ghost Lancastrian VM703 flying on the power of two Ghost jet engines with the Merlins stopped.

![Ghost Lancastrian VM703 in flight]

Comet 3 prototype G-ANLO.

DH.110 WG236, first flown by John on 26 September 1951.

Comet 1 prototype G-5-1/G-ALVG's maiden flight on 27 July 1949.

Canadian Pacific Airways Comet 1A CF-CUN in doorway of new aluminium flight test hangar during construction. This aircraft crashed at Karachi on 3 March 1953 during delivery flight, stalling during the take-off run.

Trident 1 G-ARPA, first flown by John 9 January 1962.

The recovered parts were taken to the RAE at Farnborough for the most detailed and searching aircraft accident investigation ever undertaken, led by the Royal Aircraft Establishment under Sir Arnold Hall. A special rig was constructed to allow the aircraft remains to be reassembled to demonstrate how the aircraft had broken up and to determine the location of the weak link. In parallel to this reconstruction, a fully instrumented Comet 1A (G-ANAV) was test flown from the RAE by John Cunningham and RAE Aero Flight test pilot Roger Topp to check the possibility of flutter in the airframe which could have caused it to disintegrate. The testing progressed gradually, methodically approaching the possible areas of catastrophic flutter, but none was found. This Comet had been flown to Farnborough on 24 May 1954 to be equipped with extensive strain gauges and instrumentation and was flown unpressurised.

In addition, Comet 1 G-ALYU was installed in a water tank at Farnborough where it was subjected to dynamic pressure testing, together with simulated flight loads until there was a failure in the cabin. The reconstructed airframe was found to have failed at the top of the cabin, where fatigue cracks had propagated between the two DF aerial rectangular cut-outs. White paint from the roof was found on the upper surfaces of the outer section of the wing. The water test tank tests on G-ALYU caused the corner of a square cabin window cut-out to fail, again due to metal fatigue. The aircraft had made 1,230 pressure flights before being installed in the test tank, and the cabin failed after a further 1,830 simulated flights. Comet 1 G-ALYP had failed after 1,290 pressure flights and G-ALYY only completed 900 flights, demonstrating a wide scatter, most likely caused by variations in structures caused by material specifications and methods of manufacture. Some wreckage of G-ALYY was salvaged by a fishing boat after the inquiry.

Following the completion of the investigation, a Court of Inquiry was convened in London from 19 October until 24 November 1954, with the resulting report issued on 12 February 1955. The early part of the report dealt with the design philosophy of the Comet based on

current knowledge and practice. Structural testing by de Havilland
had exceeded the British Civil Airworthiness Requirements (BCAR).
The airworthiness authorities found that the company had done all
it could to protect against fatigue cracking, and possible failure of
any window, door, or hatch. The entire aircraft had been designed in
excess of current requirements.

In the mid-1940s, the engineering industry was becoming aware
that static testing could not protect entirely against fatigue and that
dynamic testing was also required. As a result, de Havilland began
to test for the safe working life of the cabin by dynamically testing
another specimen which survived for so long; the safety of the Comet
cabin was established with an apparent ample margin. When testing
the pressure cabin statically, the pressure was doubled, and it still
survived. What was not understood at the time was that this extra
stress on the test specimen strengthened it metallurgically, which the
production fuselages did not benefit from. The test specimens were
not fully representative of production units as they had been hand-
made without the use of press tools and within tolerances inevitably
above the normal production specification.

The report was published widely, allowing the global aerospace
industry to benefit from the findings. No blame was placed upon
de Havilland, but the cabin windows for the new Comet 3 were
rounded to equal out the stress loads of pressurising the cabin. Work
methods were changed, particularly with the practice of dealing
with cracks detected in the skin during manufacture. If found in
an area of low stress, cracks were stopped by drilling a hole, but
repaired if continued to propagate. Cracks in high-stress areas
were repaired. To maintain a flush drag-reducing finish, instead of
counter-sinking holes in skins, spin dimpling was used to maintain
material integrity.

Most Comet 2s had their cabins re-skinned with thicker gauge
material and oval windows and the two RCAF Comet 1As were
also re-skinned for continued service with 412 Squadron. John
collected the first RCAF Comet 1A from the de Havilland Canada
factory near Toronto, having to decide whether to fly the aircraft

back to Britain for cabin modification unpressurised, or at 2.5 lb pressure, making the short flight to Winnipeg to prove the height was adequate at 25,000 feet. Following the rebuild of the fuselages at Broughton, John returned the aircraft to Canada. In addition, of the three returned Air France Comet 1As, two had the cabin strengthened with oval windows and were used as flying systems laboratories at Boscombe Down and Hatfield respectively.

Although Comet production had been halted since the accidents, development flying led by John had continued on Comet 2s and the sole Comet 3 prototype (G-ANLO), which John and Peter Bugge flew for the first time from Hatfield on 19 July 1954. Other members of the crew were Tony Fairbrother (flight test observer), Brackstone-Brown (flight engineer), and John Marshall, who became superintendent of the instrument lab in flight tests. Sufficient hours were flown to allow the Comet 3 to be demonstrated at Farnborough in September, together with a production Comet 2. By mid-November, the Comet 3 had made some fifty flights, one of the recognition features being wing leading edge pinion fuel tanks.

As well as foreign flights, there were periods of concentrated testing. In August 1954, John spent his time testing the Comet 3, as a selection of entries from his logbook demonstrates: 'Flap Buffet', 'Yungman Stall Warning', 'Engine roughness and flap buffet', 'Flaps', 'Engines & Flaps', and 'Stall Warning'. Between 3 and 5 November 1954, he made six flights, lasting a total of four hours and twenty-five minutes on 'Stalls'. In mid-March 1955, a little over a month after the Comet 1 accident report had been published, de Havilland announced the Comet 4, incorporating all the lessons learned. BOAC ordered a fleet of nineteen for their Commonwealth routes.

The Comet 3 did not have the new fuselage structure, but it was aerodynamically similar to the future Comet 4, allowing early certification of the new airliner.

Meanwhile, with the delays caused by the Comet 1 investigation, Rolls-Royce had developed more power for the Avon, taking it to 7,300 lb, which required a supplementary series of tropical trials.

Comet 2 G-AMXD was flown to Khartoum on 30 September 1954 for hot weather trials and Entebbe at 3,760 feet for hot and high take-off trials, returning to Hatfield on 7 October. These trials were part of the requirements for obtaining a C of A for passenger operation by the RAF, but at that time this aircraft did not have the strengthened fuselage. Comet sales prospects had evaporated while production was stopped, as no delivery dates, prices nor specifications could be agreed. The earlier BOAC Comet 1s were all allocated to various aspects of the investigation and like the prototypes were later scrapped.

Otherwise, test flying in 1955 was similar to the previous years, culminating in December with a long trip encircling the globe, the first for a jet aircraft. Leaving Hatfield in Comet 3 G-ANLO on 2 December, John and his team flew to Cairo, Bombay, Singapore, Darwin, Sydney, Melbourne, and Perth. They then headed to Auckland and from there to Fiji and Honolulu before landing in Vancouver. Christmas was spent in Toronto before returning to Hatfield on 28 December.

A 'press demonstration' on the 29th brought the company, the aeroplane, and the crew a great deal of good publicity. The Comet 3 flew the last transatlantic sector of 3,350 nautical miles in six hours and eight minutes—less than half the regular airline schedule. As a result of this epic operation and his contribution to jet transport, John was awarded the Harmon Trophy by President Eisenhower of the USA. The Comet 3 was able to provide detailed performance information, as well as stall testing and take-off performance, reducing development flying on the Comet 4, and allowing it to enter service sooner.

A total of fourteen Comet 2s were eventually completed at Hatfield, and one from Broughton, the majority being operated by the RAF. Two (G-AMXD and G-AMXK) were fitted with Rolls-Royce RA 29 Avon engines in the outer nacelles as part of the Comet 4 development programme, with G-AMXD being used by BOAC for route proving trials with the new more powerful engine and strengthened cabins. Both aircraft were later used as flying laboratories for long-range radio tests and autoland development respectively. The remaining thirteen Comet 2s served with the RAF, three as low pressurisation intelligence-gathering aircraft with 51 Squadron, and the other ten on regular global military passenger flights by 216 Squadron based at Lyneham. One other Comet, Series 2 prototype G-ALYT, continued as an Avon test-bed until it was flown into retirement, landing on the short grass runway at RAF Halton on 15 June 1959 with John at the controls. When the aerodynamic development of the Comet 4 was completed, G-ANLO had its outer wings replaced by reduced-span extension wings, without pinion fuel tanks, to undertake aerodynamic testing for the planned Comet 4Bs for BEA, becoming designated Comet 3B John made the first flight on 21 August 1958. When that programme was completed, the Comet 3B became XP915 and was delivered to the Blind landing Experimental Unit (BLEU) at RAE Bedford on 21 June 1961 for the development of autoland systems, finally retiring from flying at the end of 1972.

On 1 December 1958, John Cunningham was appointed to the de Havilland Aircraft Company Board. He was not only an outstanding test pilot with an analytical mind capable of solving complex flight testing challenges. He was also an excellent demonstration pilot, not only for the enjoyment of prospective customers, also at major air displays, where he could show an aircraft to the best advantage. He was also an ambassador for de Havilland and Britain, equally at ease with senior politicians and royalty of all nationalities. His modesty and knowledge gained through wide experience were appreciated. John tended to specialise in aerodynamic development, delegating much else to his talented team.

6

Comet 4

The Comet 4 was a new aircraft embodying all the knowledge of the earlier jet airliner operations. By the time it was ready for service, there was jet airliner competition from Boeing in the form of the 707 four-engined long-range airliner developed from a USAF flight refuelling tanker requirement.

The Comet's pressurised fuselage was built using a thicker-gauge fatigue-resistant aluminium alloy and production technology had to be upgraded significantly. On 17 March 1955, de Havilland announced the programme for a new world jet airliner, designated the Comet 4, with a launch order for twenty aircraft for BOAC, including the fatigue test specimen. By this time, there had been a water test tank built at Hatfield, initially for Comet 2 airframes, but capable of extension to the larger Comet 4.

In addition to the redesigned fuselage, there was increased fuel capacity and power from four Rolls-Royce RA 29 turbojets. The new variant carried fifty-eight first-class passengers up to 2,870 miles, allowing operations from London to Johannesburg with two intermediate stops. It was also possible to fly the 3,502 miles from London to New York in nine hours and thirty minutes, with an intermediate refuelling stop at Gander. The RA 29 engines gave a thrust of 10,500 lb, with an improvement in cruising fuel consumption, the maximum auw being 152,500 lb. Useable fuel capacity was increased to 8,750 gal and payload was 16,850 lb.

The new Avon engines gave a very lively take-off performance, the runway length at sea level and 30 degrees C being 2,380 yards at the all-up weight, allowing for an engine failure at a critical point during the take-off. The optimum cruising speed was the equivalent Mach 0.74 or 489 mph in standard atmosphere. The cabin layout could be varied from fifty-eight passengers, four abreast at a 40-inch pitch, to seventy-six passengers five abreast at a 38-inch pitch. The aircraft was operated by a flight crew of four—two pilots, a flight engineer, and a navigator.

By mid-1955, the preliminary performance figures were expected to improve as a result of further flight testing on the Comet 3. Practical stage lengths at full payload increased by 145 miles to 2,945 miles, by using a higher rate of climb to reduce stage time. Capacity payload for fifty-eight first-class passengers was 16,400 lb, and for seventy-six tourist-class passengers, it was 19,300 lb. This improved performance allowed the Comet 4 to fly from London to Johannesburg with one stop in an elapsed time of thirteen hours. The Comet 4 could also fly from New York to San Francisco with a full load.

Although the Comet 4 did not have full non-stop transatlantic capability, de Havilland believed that to achieve such a performance would require an aircraft too large for average worldwide services. The Comet 4 was however ideal in size and range for transcontinental South Atlantic and Pacific routes. Most of the major design programme had been completed, allowing production to start deliveries at the end of 1958.

The Comet 3 was also fitted with RA 29 Avon engines in 1956, re-flying on 13 February 1957, achieving some 80 per cent of C of A flying to be completed before the maiden flight of the Comet 4, allowing full production to be established at an early stage. Combining the flying by the Comet 2Es and Comet 3, some 4,000 hours of engine development would be completed by the time the new Comet entered service. With flight development and structural testing, the Comet 4 was the most thoroughly tried and tested airliner in existence.

With some 3,000 separate fatigue tests conducted on specimen assemblies and the fuselage, fatigue life was expected to exceed 100,000 pressurisations. A Comet 2 airframe was modified to the new structural standards of the Comet 4, as preliminary testing for both the new aircraft, and also to prove the structural integrity for operations by the RAF. Comet 2 airframe 06036 was installed in the Hatfield water tank and commenced trial runs on 26 November 1955, simulating a typical flight every four minutes. The fuselage was completely submerged in the tank and filled with water, which was pressurised to a differential of 8.25 lb, to contain any damage caused. The wings protruded out of each side with hydraulic jacks simulating typical take-off, climb, cruise, descent, and landing loads.

The tests were continued round the clock for nearly forty-eight hours simulating 1,500 flying hours, when the tank was emptied to allow inspection for damage before repeating the test. The object was to demonstrate that no fatigue cracks would appear in 60,000 simulated flights, and that any subsequent cracks would be contained within a further 60,000 reversals, giving the specimen a safe life of 180,000 flights. Allowing a safety factor of six gave an overall safe operating life of 30,000 flying hours.

The main reason for the Comet 3 around-the-world tour was to be able to study the operational performance of the aircraft, flying strictly in accordance with typical airline procedures on representative stages of familiar trade routes around the globe, through a variety of climatic conditions. The aircraft was flown in BOAC markings, and Peter Cane (who had headed the Comet 1 fleet with BOAC) shared the flying with John and Peter Bugge. When BOAC was not directly represented at an airport, the aircraft was handled by the resident airline, including Qantas, TAA, and CPA, providing additional experience.

Full opportunity was taken to demonstrate the aircraft to a number of airlines, airworthiness authorities, the media, and the public. On many of the routes, locally based airline crews participated in operation of the aircraft. The Comet 3 was highly reliable throughout the tour, the only technical fault was the attachment of the No. 3 engine jet pipe. It worked well at many airports unfamiliar with jet airliner operations. The low wing loading made the aircraft docile on the approach; the excellent power-to-weight ratio lifted the Comet away rapidly, fitting it in well with an existing runway and take-off patterns.

As part of the worldwide marketing programme, some 600 passengers experienced the unique smoothness of jet operations, despite the very basic standard of cabin furnishings. What was demonstrated was the ability of the Comet to sustain global scheduled operations with a high level of reliability and regularity.

As a result of operational experience, many major design improvements of the Comet 4 included increased flap area for better approach control. Hydraulic and electrical equipment were located in completely separate bays, and much work had been done to improve the flameproof qualities of the electrical systems. Anti-skid brakes were fitted and reverse thrust was provided in the two outboard engines, with improved jet exhausts to reduce engine noise. The flight deck was redesigned to accommodate up to five crew, and the passenger cabin could be easily adapted from first class to tourist layout, discarding the original scheme of a first-class cabin only.

In mid-1956, de Havilland announced the Comet 4A, a short to medium-haul version, with the Comet 4 still offered for longer ranges. The Comet 4A was lengthened by 40 inches to accommodate up to 95 passengers, with wing span reduced from 115 feet to 108 feet, providing high cruising speed at lower altitudes. The launch order for fourteen Comet 4As to Capital Airlines in the USA was announced on 26 July 1956. Unfortunately, Capital Airlines experienced financial difficulties, going into liquidation before any Comets could be delivered.

A year after the Comet 4A launch, de Havilland released initial details of the Comet 4B, which claimed jet speed and comfort for the same cost as contemporary turbo-props. With a fuselage stretch to 118 feet and a wingspan of 107 feet 10 inches, but with the pinion tanks removed, this aircraft in effect replaced the Comet 4A. The Comet 4B could carry 100 tourist class passengers over stages of up to 2,000 miles, but by climbing to 38,000 feet, the same payload could be carried 2,600 miles. In August 1957, BEA placed an initial order for six new Comet 4Bs to be operated on the longer Mediterranean routes from 1960.

John had played a significant role in the BEA selection of the Comet 4Bs to be followed by the later Trident. He was involved in the early discussions to determine the airline's detailed requirements, and the chairman Sholto Douglas wanted to take advantage of de Havilland's expertise and experience. Both John and Peter Bugge had been responsible for the development of night fighter operations in the Second World War, which had become the overall responsibility of Sholto Douglas after the Battle of Britain.

Publicity helped to sell aeroplanes and with the spectacular improvements in technology and performance, companies rivalled each other to break records and de Havilland was no exception. Over the course of Cunningham's career, he broke many world records. During the course of the flight development programme, Comet 3 G-ANLO broke a number of city-to-city records, two of which were within eight days. John flew the aircraft from London to Khartoum on 16 October 1957—a distance of 3,064 miles in a time of five hours and fifty-one minutes, giving an average speed of 523.4 mph. On the night of 23–24 October, the 5,634.6 miles from London to Johannesburg was covered in twelve hours, fifty-eight minutes, and fifty-seven seconds, including fifty-three minutes on the ground at Khartoum. This represented an average speed of 490 mph. Both flights were part of a programme of tropical and high-altitude trials using the power of the RA 29 Avon turbojets.

At the end of 1957, the ultimate Comet 4C was announced, combining the high density of the long fuselage Comet 4B with the long-range full span wings of the Comet 4, providing a substantially greater payload with a modest reduction in range. The Comet 4C in effect became the major export version of the airliner. By early 1958, Comet 4 production was starting at Hatfield and Broughton, with the first aircraft for BOAC (G-APDA) starting assembly in the otherwise empty erecting shop. The fuselage was brought into the line through side doors and lowered onto the wing assembly. By the time the undercarriage had been installed, the aircraft was ready to be pulled, nose up, down to the high bay at the end where assembly could be completed, systems installed, and RA 29 engines fitted. G-APDA was moved into the Experimental Department for resonance testing, after which it was pulled out and moved to the new flight test hangar to prepare for engine runs and the maiden flight.

The unique aluminium structure flight test hangar had been built in time for the early export Comet 1As in the early 1950s and was a fully integrated flight test facility, not only as a hangar for aircraft, but complete with air traffic control, fire station, laboratories, and accommodation for the test pilots, flight engineers, and flight development personnel, all under the overall control of John. This building still exists as a grade II structure and is now used as a fitness centre.

The all-new Comet 4 development programme started with John making the maiden flight from Hatfield on 27 April 1958, with the first export order coming from Aerolineas Argentinas for six Comet 4s having been announced on 19 March. Complementing the Comet 4 development flying, the two Comet 2Es were flown as part of the engine certification programme. One of the aircraft flew on long-range cruise, airborne for eight hours and six minutes, from Heathrow around Europe, landing with 900 gallons of fuel, enough for a further hour of flying. This was the longest Comet flight to date.

As a result of these trials, certification of the RA 29 was achieved with an initial overhaul life of 750 hours, followed by an extension to 1,000 hours. The two aircraft allocated to the RA 29 certification programme were G-AMXD owned by BOAC and G-AMXK owned by the Ministry of Supply, each aircraft having two 10,500-lb thrust

RA 29s in the outer nacelles, with the two standard 7,300-lb-thrust RA 9s inboard. The first phase of the programme started on 16 September 1957 and was completed on 31 May 1958 with a total of 7,000 engine hours, much of the flying being between London and Beirut with other operations to Gander and Nairobi. As the RA 29s were overpowering the aircraft, the two RA 9s were throttled back to allow the bigger engines 29s to use their full power.

On 12 September 1958, John flew G-APDA to the new 7,730-foot-long Hong Kong, Kai Tak Airport as part of the opening celebrations, making the demanding approach over the city, with a final turn at the 'checker board'. The 7,925-mile return to London was made in three stages, via Bombay (now Mumbai) and Cairo in a flying time of sixteen hours and sixteen minutes. The total elapsed time was eighteen hours and twenty-two minutes, resulting in the fastest long-range flight in airliner history up to that time.

John had already flown the Comet 4 into New York, Idlewild (now Kennedy) Airport on 11 August to measure its noise performance and compliance with the noise regulations. The return to Hatfield was made in an unofficial time of six hours and sixteen minutes. From 16 to 22 September, John and crew made a tour of Canada and South America, visiting Ottawa, Toronto, Montreal, and Vancouver. It was then flown via Mexico to Lima, Buenos Aires, Rio de Janeiro, Caracas, and back to New York. During the 23,000-mile tour, VIP passengers were carried on many demonstrations, one of the most demanding operations of the tour being a take-off from Mexico City with a full commercial load to Lima. Mexico City's elevation was 7,340 feet, the temperature was around 25 degrees, and with the main runway closed, the secondary runway of 8,200 feet was used instead.

With the full C of A achieved, the first two Comet 4s (G-APDB and G-APDC) were handed over to BOAC at their engineering base in a formal ceremony on 30 September 1958, followed by a third aircraft on 3 October, ready for commercial jet airliner operations to restart. Although the Comet 4 was designed for the empire routes through Africa, the Middle East, and to Asia, it was decided to make a spectacular start by inaugurating the world's first jet airliner transatlantic service between London and New York. A pre-inaugural press flight was flown on 2 October 1958, followed by the start of regular operations on 4 October, the aircraft used being Comet 4 G-APDC. This action beat the PanAm Boeing 707 flights by three weeks, and by 14 November, the London to New York service was operating daily, having started as a weekly service. This was the world's first regular transatlantic jet service.

In addition to demonstrating aircraft in his care to prospective customers and the travelling public, John tended to specialise in aerodynamic testing, including multiple stalls to obtain the safest possible handling in service, although it is a manoeuvre which passengers would not expect to experience. John's analytical approach was to approach a flight regime in very small increments with a great deal of patience, finally pushing the performance and handling boundaries close to their limits. This allowed the normal operating flying of the aircraft to be defined, well inside the extremes of the flight envelope boundaries.

John and his team were responsible for flight development of the subsequent Comet 4B and 4C developments, the latter achieving American FAA certification as the initial sale was to Mexicana. In addition to development flying, all Comets off the production lines at Hatfield and Broughton were flown to a clearly defined test schedule, and any snags cleared and checked, before offering the aircraft for customer acceptance, both on the ground and in the air. There could then be a series of customer crew training flights, initially at Hatfield, and then a visit to the airline base, where further training would make pilots aware of the local air traffic requirements and allow the engineers to practise their training. If it was an early delivery to an airline, John and his team would then train the crews on typical routes, usually wearing an airline captain's uniform, until they were happy about the crews' skills.

Comet 4s were sold to East African Airways, operated in conjunction with BOAC. Comet 4Bs were operated by Olympic in conjunction with BEA. Comet 4Cs were sold to United Arab

Airlines, later Misrair; Middle East Airlines based in Beirut; Sudan Airways, one of which was the last Comet to be built at Hatfield; and Kuwait Airways, preceding their Tridents. Many of the global fleet of Comets were later to be acquired by Dan-Air for inclusive-tour operations to Mediterranean resorts. Another major operator was the RAF which ordered five Comet C.4s, in addition to the earlier Comet C.2s, also for operation by 216 Squadron on worldwide routes. John was very much involved with the production testing of the RAF Comet C.4s, based on the Comet 4C. The aircraft were also used for long-range services for the royal family, government ministers, and RAF VIPs. Pat Fillingham undertook much of the crew training, initially from Hatfield, and then from Lyneham, before the availability of sophisticated flight simulators. This often involved the training captain standing at the rear of the flight deck monitoring the trainee pilots under instruction.

Among the airlines that John trained was Kuwait Airways, where one of the junior first officers was Ian Whittle, son of jet engine pioneer Sir Frank Whittle. The initial introduction was on a cold January day in 1963, when the chief pilot, Captain Hebborn, and Ian were waiting in their smart uniforms for the roll-out of their first Comet 4C. The airline management and John were in attendance. John's duties were to captain the aircraft on its acceptance flight, then take it on its delivery through the Middle East to Kuwait, with stops at Beirut and Cairo. Captain Hebborn and Ian took it in turns to sit in the right-hand seat to gain familiarisation with the autopilot and avionics, and being briefed by John on the Comet flight characteristics. John completed Ian's flying training at Beirut in early 1963.

Airliners configured as exotic business jets are common nowadays, but a converted Comet 4C was the first-ever jet airliner business jet. It was ordered by King Ibn Saud of Saudi Arabia as SA-R-7 and fitted out with its luxury interior at Hatfield. It was first flown from Hatfield on 29 March 1962, and sadly demonstrated that even in modern relatively low-risk times, accidents can happen. The project crew for this aircraft were Captain John Hanslip and flight engineer

Ken Rouse, their major task being to train the American crews. The first visit to its potential operating base in Jeddah was in August 1962, before formal base crew training started from Hatfield in late September through most of October. Crew training continued with route proving around Europe and occasional visits to Saudi Arabia.

On 19 March, SA-R-7 departed Hatfield for Geneva, and then operated a shuttle between Nice and Geneva, with King Saud and his retinue on board for the first of three round trips. On the third flight, with the American crew close to being finally cleared, the de Havilland crew of John Hanslip and Ken Rouse were resting in the cabin after a very long operational period. In the early hours of 20 March, the aircraft struck a ridge close to the top of the Alps near Cuneo, killing all on board. The aircraft was so close to the top that some of the wreckage went over the ridge. Peter Bugge, John's deputy, was given the task of joining the accident investigation team and visiting the almost inaccessible site of the wreckage.

Comet 4s were the basis of the Nimrod maritime reconnaissance aircraft for the RAF. The last two unsold Comet 4Cs on the Broughton production line were converted by having their fuselages shortened to the original Comet 4's cabin length. The first RA 29-powered prototype was flown by John and Jimmy Harrison from Hawarden to Woodford on 25 October 1965. After conversion to Nimrod configuration, it flew again on 31 July 1967, still powered by the Avon engines. The second aircraft (XV148) was converted at Broughton, complete with Rolls-Royce Spey engines and made the first flight to Woodford on 23 May 1967.

The last Comet 4 to fly was 4C XS235, which was delivered to the A&AEE at Boscombe Down on 2 December 1963 as a flying laboratory. On 20 July 1996 was the last time John handled an aircraft—Comet 4C XS235 from Boscombe Down. Nearly half a century had flown past since his maiden flight of the Comet 1. After flying the Comet 4C, he declined all invitations to take the pilot's seat, saying, 'sorry, I'm not current'. This aircraft was finally retired to Bruntingthorpe on 30 October 1997, where it is maintained in running order.

7

Trident

The Trident second-generation airliner was the last full flight development programme headed by John Cunningham. At the same time, he had responsibility for the DH.125 business jet flight testing. John's test pilot team consisted of himself, with Peter Bugge his deputy. Pat Fillingham was still involved, with Ron Clear, who had moved from the Airspeed Division at Christchurch. Jimmy Phillips was the project pilot for the Trident Autoland programme; other Trident test pilots were Peter Barlow and Des Penrose, both ex-Sea Vixen pilots.

The project test pilot for the DH.125 was Chris Capper, who had tested Sea Vixens at Christchurch, together with Geoffrey Pike, who had previously made the maiden flights of the Dove, Vampire night fighter, and Heron. Directly working for John was also a team of flight engineers. Responsible under John for missile testing at the de Havilland Propeller Company on the Manor Road side of the aerodrome were Don Lucey, Bob Sowray (who later joined the DH.125 team), and George Aird (who eventually took over the production test flying at Hawarden).

Just down the corridor from the test pilots was the flight development team headed by Tony Fairbrother, who had been part of the original Comet 1 maiden flight team. John was also responsible for managing air traffic, aerodrome services, and management. There were also Alan Brandon and Tony Chalke at Hawarden, test pilot and flight test observer, but for Comet testing and delivery to Hatfield, a crew from Hatfield would attend. In addition, there was a communications fleet based at Hatfield, consisting of three Doves, a Heron, and whatever DH.125s were available.

At each HSA airfield (Dunsfold, Brough, and Woodford), Doves were based for local site communications, co-ordinated from Hatfield, where all the head office requests for air transport were directed. There was a daily service between Hatfield and Hawarden, initially operated by eight-seat Dove G-ALBM, often flown by Reggie Moon, who was formally a flying instructor at Panshanger, and later fourteen-seat Heron G-AVTI, the last off the Broughton production line. There were additional demonstration pilots including Mike Maina, Ron Wakely, and Steven Cherry-Downes, who would fly communications operations as well as demonstrations to potential customers.

John therefore headed a significant organisation, as well as continuing to undertake regular test flying, both at home and overseas. His secretary and PA between them covered day-to-day administration, which included running the company communications aircraft fleet and making sure all the flights were fully crewed.

At times also based at Hatfield were Sea Vixens for development in their FAW.2 form, as well as missile testing from the Manor Road side of the aerodrome. There was also Beaver 2 G-ANAR, Cirrus Moth G-EBLV, and from time to time the Hawarden-based Mosquito T.III RR299, which was flown by Pat Fillingham, Ron Clear, Chris Capper, and occasionally John Cunningham. Also flying with the Propeller Company on missile development were Canberras and Lightnings and the last Comet 1A XM823, which was delivered into preservation at Shawbury on 8 April 1968, now in the RAF Museum at Cosford.

In its heyday, the de Havilland Engine Company operated such exotic types as Gyron test-bed Short Sperrin, Avro Ashton, Gyron

Junior test-bed Canberra, Spectre rocket-development Canberra, and Buccaneer S.1 for Gyron Junior flight testing. Being only 20 miles from the centre of London, Hatfield aerodrome was a popular destination for the customer Doves, Herons, and DH.125s as well as a number of RAF and FAA aircraft. Later, there was to be an active Hatfield Aviation Centre for a range of business jet operators, but this ceased on the eventual closure of the aerodrome in 1993.

John would also fly sales demonstration communications flights. Sadly, when taking off from Dunsfold on 20 November 1975 with some Chinese passengers, his DH.125-600 (G-ACUX) was hit by a flock of birds, which caused both Viper engines to fail. On touching down and crossing the boundary road, they unknowingly hit a car, killing the occupants, who turned out to be the wife, two daughters, and three friends of Dick Whittingham, one of the Dunsfold test pilots who was on airfield duty at the time. John was taken to hospital with some back injuries, and he was visited later that evening by Dick to tell him what had happened. The car could only be identified by its number plate.

The Trident was a BEA requirement for a 100-seat regional jet airliner issued in 1956. As an interim, BEA ordered six Comet 4Bs, later increasing to fourteen. The order was placed in September 1957 for service entry in April 1960. The BEA requirement was for a jet airliner with more than two engines, preferably rear-mounted to reduce cabin noise and to leave the wings unobstructed for improved lift. The range was to be 1,000 miles, and the speed to be greater than existing Comets and French Caravelles.

With the disastrous 4 April 1957 Defence White Paper presented by Defence Minister Duncan Sandys, many of the manned combat aircraft projects were cancelled in favour of guided missiles. The government favoured a consolidation of the British aircraft industry, resulting in a complete reliance in civil projects. The government considered de Havilland resources insufficient to support the new BEA airliner programme, favouring Avro with the backing of the Hawker Siddeley Group. As a result, de Havilland set up Airco (Aircraft Manufacturing Company) in conjunction with Hunting and Fairey to design, develop, and manufacture the DH.121. The majority share was held by de Havilland with 67.5 per cent, Hunting 22.5 per cent, and Fairey 10 per cent.

Although the government favoured a Bristol/Hawker Siddeley competing bid, BEA much preferred the Airco offering, particularly with de Havilland Comet experience. Following much discussion, in August 1958, the minister of transport and civil aviation agreed a BEA order for twenty-four DH.121s. It had grown to a 111-seat second-generation airliner with a range of 2,000 miles, powered by three 13,500-lb thrust Rolls-Royce Medway bypass engines grouped in the rear fuselage.

In May 1959, BEA made radical changes to the specification as it was believed the original passenger capacity was over-optimistic by some 20 per cent, requiring the new airliner to have the same performance as the original project, but the overall weight reduced from 123,000 lb to 100,000 lb with a maximum seating of eighty passengers. BEA said that the design could later be stretched as extra capacity was required, but the rear engine configuration restricted power as the centre engine location was limited in size.

With the reliance on civil aviation to survive, as de Havilland had lost work within the 1957 Defence White Paper, the consortium was forced to revise the design to comply with one customer's requirements. In effect, the maximum weight was reduced to 105,000 lb with passenger capacity reduced to a maximum of 100. Power was to come from three 9,850-lb thrust Rolls-Royce Spey bypass jets yet to be developed. The overall project had 40 per cent less thrust, range reduced by half, and 20 per cent less passenger capacity, reducing drastically the global sales opportunities for the aircraft. The competing Boeing 727 was similar in size to the original DH.121, selling a total of 1,387 aircraft, compared with 117 Tridents. Within three years of downsizing, BEA executives realised the reduction had been unnecessary and the original project had been the correct size. The major problem with the Trident was its lack of power, but its major asset was its very efficient wing.

A contract for twenty-four DH.121s was awarded to de Havilland by BEA on 12 August 1959, with financial aid by the government to cover launching aid. With its three engines and triplicated systems, the DH.121 was appropriately named Trident in August 1960. It was to be capable of full automatic landing. With the government policy of encouraging mergers of the much-fragmented British aircraft companies in the late 1950s, de Havilland Airco would be the basis of a third group after Hawker Siddeley Group—by far the largest with Avro, Hawker, Armstrong Whitworth, and the planned British Aircraft Corporation as a merger of Bristol, Vickers, and English Electric. However, this was rejected by the minister of civil aviation, resulting in a merger of de Havilland with Hawker Siddeley. On 17 December 1959, the Boards of Hawker Siddeley and de Havilland announced that the two companies would be merged into Hawker Siddeley Aviation, the other members of Airco going into separate groups.

The Trident was designed with three autopilots and three hydraulic systems, and if one failed, it was outvoted by the remaining pair. Full power controls were provided without manual reversion, each operated by three jacks and each served by a different hydraulic system. The development of initially autoflare to be developed into full autoland was a major advance, much preliminary research work being done at RAE Bedford with BLEU using Comets. Trident structure was traditional aluminium alloy, and the first aircraft (G-ARPA) was assembled in the high bay at the end of the erecting shop, the final Comet 4C for Sudanair having to be edged out a side door. With the engines in the rear fuselage, there was an aerodynamically clean wing and the tailplane was mounted on the top of the fin in a 'T-tail' layout.

The two podded Speys had reverse thrust, which could be used on the approach to increase the rate of descent and reduce the landing run on touch down. As with the earlier Comets, a Trident fatigue testing airframe was installed in the Hatfield water tank, the structure being designed as a fail-safe. The Trident structure was designed to a maximum life of 20,000 flights each of ninety minutes.

A Trident systems 'iron bird' was built in technical services, where the triplicated systems were tested for endurance and serviceability. An analogue simulator was integrated with the systems testing, allowing the design of the flight deck to be established. John Wilson, having retired from test flying, was the main operator, working closely with John Cunningham. While 'flying' this rig, some elevator over-sensitivity was discovered in the approach to land mode, and a simple modification was introduced to overcome the problem before flight trials began.

All Tridents were assembled at Hatfield, and the wing/fuselage centre-section, rear fuselage, and fin were also made there. Factories within Hawker Siddeley Aviation manufactured other assemblies, including the nose and forward fuselage at Portsmouth until the site was closed in 1968. The former Blackburn factory at Brough took over this work and the former Folland factory at Hamble built the wings and tailplanes.

The first Trident 1 (G-ARPA) was rolled out at Hatfield on 4 August 1961, fitted with only two ground-running Speys. Many systems needed completion and installation of flight test instrumentation. After initial engine runs, slow taxying trials tested the effectiveness of the offset nose undercarriage, which had been designed to retract sideways to save space in equipment bays. The main undercarriage was also unique as it featured four wheels on one axle, and twisted through 90 degrees to tuck into the wing to fuselage joint. A feature of this undercarriage was the fairly hard ride over the joints in concrete surfaces.

The aircraft was cleared for flight on 21 December to the schedule agreed two years earlier, but the maiden flight was delayed due to a heavy fall of snow, which was cleared by 8 January allowing John to make some test hops down the runway. The following day, John took the Trident off for the first time with Peter Bugge as number two and Braxtone-Brown, also known as 'Brax', as chief flight engineer, plus Tony Fairbrother, John Johnstone, and Ron Marshall, on a one-hour twenty-minute test flight.

Watched by Sir Geoffrey, the Trident was airborne after 3,000 feet of the 6,000-foot runway, and a pair of chase aircraft kept the

Trident company. Things did not quite go to plan. Not revealed to the press after the flight was that the undercarriage sequencing valve malfunctioned when one of the main undercarriage legs retracted. As the main undercarriage doors opened, one failed, while the other came down correctly. Des Penrose in the Canberra chase plane reported this malfunction to the Trident crew. The critical situation was corrected by Brax, who switched off the hydraulic system controlling the undercarriage, allowing the door to open and the undercarriage leg to come down, locking itself in the free fall.

It was known that the high tail configuration could lead to an unrecoverable deep stall. The delta wing Gloster Javelin all-weather fighter had suffered from this phenomenon resulting in the loss of pilot and aircraft. During the testing of a BAC One-Eleven on 22 October 1963, a deep stall has been experienced, with the aircraft falling in a deep stall almost vertically over Salisbury Plain, killing the crew including Mike Lithgow, BAC chief test pilot. In effect the wing blanketed airflow to the high tailplane and the engine air intakes, precluding any increase in power to recover. The requirement was to fly the Trident as close to the stall as possible without entering that flight regime, and a stick shaker was fitted to warn the pilot of the approach to the stall. If that was ignored, a stick pusher forced the nose down in the unlikely situation where an airline pilot might become close to losing control. John was in charge of establishing the stall safety boundaries.

Five Tridents were allocated to the flight development programme, G-ARPA being used for low- and high-speed handling and structural load measurements; G-ARPB for performance and system testing, including autopilot development into a full autoland capability; G-ARPC for additional low-speed handling and performance measurements powered by production Speys and certification flying; G-APRD was fitted with wing leading-edge slats instead of droop leading edges as on the improved Trident 1E; and G-ARPE for BEA acceptance checks and route proving flights.

Assistance in this intensive programme came from senior BEA captains, including Mike Mitchell, John Johnson, and Eric Poole, the latter assisting Jimmy Phillips with the automatic landing development.

The second Trident (G-ARPB) was also used early on for tropical trials with a flight test team led by John. The first of three series was to Torrejón in Spain and Khartoum in November 1962. This aircraft had flown on 20 May 1962. The second series was to Torrejón again and Cairo in late September 1963, and finally Djibouti in February 1966.

G-ARPA's initial assessment was good: trials measuring airfield and climb performance, simulated engine failure on take-off, and nose-high take-offs with the rear fuselage protected against damage by a wooden skid, to ensure that the aircraft would not stall on the ground during take-off. The use of reverse thrust at all altitudes up to maximum operating speed was cleared. To create additional drag to facilitate descent, the main undercarriage could be lowered below speeds of 300 kt, but in practice, this was not used in case the pilots believed the full undercarriage was lowered and inadvertently landed with the nose wheel retracted. This Trident spent the first eight months mainly on low-speed handling trials to overcome problems with the wing leading edge droop configuration, followed by flutter testing.

Trident low-speed performance was initially unsatisfactory because of early flow separation over the outer wings, and there was no clear definition of a nose drop close to the stall with full flaps selected. Finally, a Kruger flap was fitted at the wing root leading edge, but the shape and sealing of the wing droop, vortex generators, and wing fence position required many flights to achieve a satisfactory performance. Each trial consisted of building up the profile with ply, balsa wood, and sealant, using wool tufts on the wings to assess the results. More than 3,000 stalls were flown to ensure characteristics acceptable to the airworthiness authorities and to confirm that a stick pusher would have to be fitted. The stick pusher was activated by two vanes, one on each side of the cockpit exterior; when the aircraft reached a 17-degree incidence with the droop leading edge down, or 11 degrees clean, the stick pusher would pitch the nose down with an 80-lb force.

John's dedication to achieving good handling qualities was demonstrated by a page of his logbook for the period 26 April to 15 May 1962, detailing twenty-three flights of which twenty-two were in Trident G-ARPA with the laconic comment 'Stalls' amounting to sixteen hours and fifteen minutes of flying time. From 19–23 July, he recorded seven flights carrying out stalls on the Trident.

Following the protracted slow-speed handling development, G-ARPA was then used for high-speed trials, achieving a remarkable Mach 0.96, which was better than the prediction of Mach 0.95. This positive result allowed a speed certification to Mach 0.88, equivalent to 610 mph at 25,000 feet. G-ARPA had reached Mach 0.96 in a shallow dive between 30,000 and 24,000 feet, equivalent to 652 and 667 mph, making the Trident the fastest jet airliner in service. Handling and control were pleasant and positive throughout the entire flight envelope.

G-ARPE was close to production standard and John took it on a sales demonstration and route proving tour to Japan in October 1963 to All Nippon Airways with demonstrations in Tokyo, Hong Kong, Singapore, Karachi, and Damascus. In the event, All Nippon followed Japan Air Lines in ordering Boeing 727s. The Trident returned to Hatfield on 29 October surrounded by five production and development aircraft on the apron. At least the tour was not a complete waste as Tridents were later ordered by Pakistan International Airways (PIA). By mid-1963, total Trident flight development time had reached 1,000 hours, with production standard Speys becoming available, and a further 200 hours of route proving on BEA routes, including a Middle East sales tour in January 1964, which resulted in sales to Iraqi Airways and Kuwait Airways.

The flight development Tridents were flown to Bitteswell near Coventry to bring them up to production standard, and G-ARPB was leased back to Hatfield in June 1964 to start three and a half years of autoland development. During this programme, some 2,300 hours were flown, of which just under 1,600 were directly involved with testing. Although it was hoped that the Trident would be in

BEA service by early 1964, it had been delayed by the low-speed handling difficulties, the C of A being awarded on 18 February 1964, followed by service entry on 11 March.

The Trident and Autoland

The pioneering development of automatic landing in all weathers was led by what had then become Hawker Siddeley Aviation, with the well-established Hatfield flight development team. John appointed gifted test pilot Jimmy Phillips, one of the youngest pilots in his early thirties as project pilot, working with Smiths Industries and the Hatfield design team, to certificate fully automatic landings in all weathers, creating a certainty of arriving at the final destination and avoiding expensive and annoying diversions. The Hatfield development of automatic landing in all weathers was probably as big a pioneering achievement as anything since the original development of the jet airliner. Such a capability is part of the computerised flight management systems of all modern jet airliners.

The Blind Landing Experimental Unit (BLEU) was formed in 1945, initially at Woodbridge, but moved the following year to Martlesham Heath. The task for the multi-disciplined team from RAE Farnborough, Telecommunications Research Establishment (TRE) at Malvern was to develop a blind approach and landing system for RAF, FAA, and civil aircraft. The BLEU system used guidance by radio signals from an early instrument landing system (ILS), which defined the extended runway centre line, and a 3-degree glide slope approach to the runway threshold. Initially, a magnetic leader cable was used for azimuth guidance during the final approach, with a radio altimeter providing height guidance during the final flare aircraft speed was controlled by automatic throttle.

Initially, the major components were tried on different aircraft with the entire system coming together for the first time in a Devon, making the first autoland on 3 July 1950. Further tests were undertaken in a Canberra as part of a military requirement for the RAF V-Force, a requirement for which was issued in 1954. The first fully automatic approach and landing in clear weather conditions was made in the larger Varsity WF417 at Martlesham Heath on 11 November 1954, with the BLEU moving to RAE Bedford at Thurleigh in early 1957. By October 1958, all BLEU aircraft had completed over 2,000 fully automatic landings, with the Vulcan system being accepted for military service in 1961.

The safety level required for military purposes was a failure rate no greater than 1 in 120,000 landings, with a single-channel system being adequate, allowing a pilot to take control in the event of a failure to either land or overshoot. This test programme was monitored by civil airlines, resulting in close co-operation between BLEU, the UK Air Registration Board (ARB), the aviation industry, and airlines. It led to the ARB defining the safety requirement for Autoland as no more than one fatal accident in 10 million. This was ten times better than was being achieved by pilots landing manually.

To achieve this much-increased level of safety, a 'triplex' system was developed with a fault system being disconnected by the other two if they disagreed. For civil applications, the leader cable would not be practical, with the ILS localiser being considerably improved throughout the 1950s. By the early 1960s, ILS transmitters had improved enough for the leader cable to be no longer required, and a new up-to-date ILS system was installed at Hatfield, complemented by a non-precision surveillance radar. As part of the build-up of the automatic landing development before flying it in the Trident, Comet 2R XV144, formerly G-AMXK, was fitted out by Smiths Industries. Comet 3 XP915 (ex-G-ANLO) was added to the BLEU fleet and XV144 was fitted with the full triplex system in 1966.

Following early flight testing with Trident G-ARPB over 600 development approaches, Jimmy Phillips made the first autoland at RAE Bedford on 3 March 1964. A demonstrate flight for journalists was made on 3 June 1965, again by Jimmy Phillips, with Captain Eric Poole nine fully automatic approaches performed at Gatwick. Only one week later, G-ARPR made the first automatic landing at

Paris carrying passengers in good visibility. The first low-visibility arrival was made at Heathrow on 4 November 1965, when the airport was closed to all other flying due to thick fog. The Trident 1 autoland development programme, involving over 2,000 landings, was completed to Cat III standard in January 1967, with BEA starting to use autoland in May 1967 with 300 autolandings being made every month. In February 1969, the airline was cleared to operate down to Cat II weather minima, which was equivalent to 200 to 100 feet decision height and 1,800 to 1,000m runway visual range (rvr), later improving to Cat IIIA limits of no decision height and rvr of 200m.

Similarly, Trident 2 G-AVFA was used for autoland trials from July 1968 to April 1969 when over 170 flying hours, Cat IIIA clearance was achieved, and the extension to Cat IIIB standards with no decision height and rvr of between 200 and 50 m for both Trident 1s and 2s. The final limit was the captain's ability to taxi visually from the gate to and from the runway. Autoland trials were completed on Trident 3 G-AWYZ from late 1970 through 1971 to Cat IIIA minima, which were increased to Cat IIIB after 5,000 recorded approaches.

Even to the experienced test pilot, the superstall could catch out the unprepared. With production of the original Trident 1 order for BEA almost complete, and export 1Es coming off the line, G-ARPY was ready for its first production test flight on a sunny Friday afternoon, 3 June 1966. Peter Barlow was captain, with former Airspeed chief test pilot George Errington in the second seat. Edgar (Brax) Braxtone-Brown, the chief flight engineer, was responsible for ensuring the aircraft was ready for flight, and Charles Paterson was the radio officer.

The object of a first production test flight was to check all systems and that handling was to specification, among which was the operation of the stall recovery system, including stick shaker and stick pusher. With incorrect handling, the Trident could enter a deep stall from which there would be no recovery. With a small number of Tridents exhibiting a wing drop close to stick pusher operation, tests for this were eventually introduced at the stall. Following stall tests with stick shaker and stick pusher, and a careful log of speeds at which they operated, both stick shaker and stick pusher were switched off. The approach to the stall used a carefully calibrated air speed indicator, to ensure accuracy. At 3 to 4 knots below the speed of their programmed operation, the pilot was immediately to recover from the stall. Peter Barlow had flown around 1,600 hours on Tridents and taken part in 2,195 stalls, of which 750 were in command.

The Trident was flown over its typical East Anglian test route, with good telemetry reception at Hatfield. Around 6.30 p.m. towards the end of the test schedule, three approaches were made to the stall with the aircraft in the landing configuration, the stall recovery systems were fully operative, followed by one stall with them switched off. The inquiry found that Peter Barlow delayed the recovery from the stall, and that the aircraft entered a deep stall from which it was impossible to recover. At 6.34 p.m., Peter radioed 'am in a deep stall—stand-by'. The aircraft fell near Felthorpe, killing the crew.

Following the loss of this Trident, John flew another the next day to get close to reproducing the conditions of the loss of 'PY. He wanted to understand as fully as possible what had happened, so that there would be no repeat. One of Cunningham's colleagues recalled that during testing of the Trident close to super stall attitude, they had a particularly difficult but ultimately successful recovery. This was typical of his calm, analytical approach to test flying.

The first development of the Trident 1 was the 1E, first announced in August 1962, in an attempt to make the aircraft more attractive in the export market. The wing span was increased by 5 feet to improve airfield performance, the flap area was increased, and wing leading edge slats replaced the earlier droop. Power came from 11,400-lb thrust Spey 511s, and fuel capacity was increased, resulting in higher operating weight and payload for minimal increase in empty weight. Payload range was improved, and although take-off and landing performance were not much different to that of the earlier 1C, hot and high climb performance was much improved. The previously located auxiliary power unit (APU) in the Trident 1C belly was moved to a much more practical location in the rear fuselage at the base of the rudder. The cabin design was improved, allowing more passengers to be carried.

John made the maiden flight of the first Trident 1E with the temporary registration G-ASWU on 2 November 1964, the flight development programme being completed without delay. During high-speed trials, the Trident 1E achieved Mach 0.975 in almost level flight. John led the trials team, including Peter Bugge and Tony Fairbrother, on tropical trials at Torrejón from 19 March to 25 March 1965, followed by additional trials in Africa, the Middle East, and Pakistan, starting with a record-breaking flight to Cairo.

The second Trident 1E (G-ASWV) was also involved in tropical trials in Nairobi and Madrid in July 1965, then Beirut in September. Both initial Trident 1Es were delivered to Kuwait Airways, who also ordered a third. Hawker Siddeley approved a production batch of fifteen Trident 1Es for the Middle East market, where Hatfield had a good reputation, as the 1E was very competitive with the larger Boeing 727, with lower purchase and operating costs. In the event, the expected number of sales was not achieved. Three Trident 1Es were sold to Iraqi Airways and four to Pakistan International Airlines (PIA). John and his team were also involved in crew training for these airlines, including route proving. The first Trident 1E was delivered to Iraqi Airways on 3 October 1965 for operations out of Baghdad. The aircraft was withdrawn from use in 1977.

John piloted the first PIA Trident 1E (AP-ATK) on delivery with an HSA and PIA crew from Heathrow via Beirut on 2 March 1966, then on to Karachi. PIA ordered Tridents for their Karachi to Peking service as the airline wanted to avoid a spares embargo from the USA if the Boeing 727 had been used. The fourth Pakistan Trident (AP-AUG) was painted in Pakistan Air Force markings, but eventually reverted to PIA colours. As traffic to China increased, the Tridents were replaced by Boeing 707s; the Tridents were sold to

CAAC of China in 1970, resulting soon after in significant orders for Trident 2s.

The first Trident 1E for Kuwait Airways was handed over at Hatfield on 18 March 1966, when the order for a third aircraft was announced. Both surviving aircraft were acquired by BEA in 1972, one having been written off in a non-fatal accident. The remaining five Trident 1Es were ordered by Channel Airways, who took only two before going into liquidation. Two of the remainder went to BKS, later Northeast at Newcastle. The final one was delivered to Ceylon Airways as 4R-ACN on 16 July 1969 where John was responsible for crew training. After suffering damage, it became an instructional airframe by April 1984 and was later scrapped.

Trident 2

With the built-in limitations caused by the BEA specification for the Trident 1, there was a need for an improved version with more powerful engines. Increased fuel and aerodynamic refinements, including greater wingspan, resulted in the Trident 2E, with a capability of flying London to Beirut direct with full payload. BEA ordered fifteen Trident 2Es with options on a further ten on 5 August 1965, with deliveries starting in 1968. The 2E was a further development of the 1E with the gross weight increased by 8,500 lb to 143,500 lb, more powerful Spey 25 engines with 11,930 lb thrust, and an additional 350-gallon fuel tank located in the fin. Aerodynamic refinements to the wing reduced drag by fitting Kuchemann wing tips, increasing span by 5 feet. John took the first BEA Trident 2 (G-AVFA) for its maiden flight from Hatfield on 27 July 1967.

Initial testing included nose-high take-offs at maximum weight with the wooden tail block on the ground, stalling clearance and flutter testing up to Mach 0.95. Then with production standard Spey 25s fitted, John with a total team of thirty-two personnel departed Hatfield on 5 November for the warmer climes of Nairobi for hot and high tests, going on to Port Darwin, returning on 6 December. On return to Hatfield, the aircraft was fitted with a long nose probe for high-speed trials exceeding Mach 0.95 on several occasions and reaching Mach 0.97, with no handling problems, despite being so close to Mach 1.

Following these aerodynamic and performance tests, G-AVFA was retained by Hawker Siddeley for 170 hours of autoland trials from June 1968 until May 1969, becoming the penultimate Trident 2E to be delivered to BEA on 5 June 1969. The second Trident 2E (G-AVFB) was used for some systems testing, followed by air conditioning trials. Trident 2s entered service with BEA on an *ad hoc* basis from London to Milan on17 April 1968, with regular operations starting on 1 June, by which time four aircraft had been delivered. Two Trident 2Es were also ordered by Cyprus Airways, operated in conjunction with BEA, the first delivery being on 18 September 1969. Cyprus Airways ceased operations when Turkey invaded the island in July 1974.

Trident 3

In mid-1964, BEA published a requirement for a 150–200-seat 'Air Bus' as a short-range aircraft for high-density routes such as London to Manchester, Paris, and Amsterdam. Hawker Siddeley proposed the HS 132, which was a lengthened two Rolls-Royce RB 178 turbofan-powered aircraft with a capacity for 180 passengers, or as an alternative, a much cheaper-to-develop 135-seat Trident 3. For BEA, the Trident 3 was regarded as too small, while the HS 132 was the right size but too costly to develop, even though the airline declared a preference for a British aircraft, also considering a short-range version of the VC-10.

In 1966, when Air France ordered 148-seat Boeing 727-200s, BEA apparently panicked and proposed an order for a mixed fleet of Boeing 727 and 737s; as a nationalised airline, it required government approval, which was withheld. BAC offered the Two-

Eleven, an enlarged BAC 1-11, with accommodation for 170 to 190 passengers, but the £60 million development costs were considered too much. BEA ended up with a combined order for Trident 3s and stretched BAC 1-11s. The Trident 3B turned out to be a logical and inexpensive development of the aircraft already in BEA service, and it had 60 per cent more payload than the Trident 1, with only a 20 per cent increase in operating weight and 25 per cent greater range. The airline also had the benefits of common training, engineering, crewing, and spares holdings.

BEA accepted that it had to order Trident 3Bs, but demanded compensation from the government as it had not been able to buy aircraft of choice. The BEA order for twenty-six Trident 3Bs was at £83 million, the largest ever for civil airliners received by the British aircraft industry. The Trident 3B had a fuselage extension of 8 feet and 5 inches forward of the wing centre-section, and 8 feet aft of the wing, providing enough accommodation for up to 146 passengers in a mixed-class layout or 180 in all economy.

Aerodynamic changes were relatively small with wing incidence increased by 2 degrees to maintain ground clearance during rotation for take-off. Span and area of the wing trailing flaps was increased to keep approach speed and landing distance acceptable, and air brakes were used as spoilers. Power for this heavier aircraft came from three 11,960-lb Speys augmented by a Rolls-Royce RB 162 5,230-lb thrust booster engine in the tail, taking the place of the APU, which was relocated on top of the centre engine air intake.

With the RB 162 in operation, the Trident 3B had a 1,500-foot shorter take-off run than the 2E, despite an increase in weight of 6,500 lb. The RB. 162 was based on vertical jet engine technology, using a part composite construction, but was extremely noisy, and had to be shut down after take-off when over the departing airport boundary.

The first Trident 3B (G-AWYZ) was rolled out at Hatfield on 17 November 1969 and was involved in resonance and other ground tests, before John and his team took it into the air for the first time on 11 December for two hours and fifty minutes, but a booster engine was not fitted; the first booster take-off was made from RAE Bedford on 26 March 1970. G-AWYZ was used for general handling, high-speed trials, development of booster performance, and autoland development.

The second aircraft (G-AWZA) flew on 9 March and was allocated to low-speed handling and stalling. Although the third aircraft was planned to be used for flight development, the 500-hour test and certification went so well that only the first two were used. From August to September 1970, G-AWYZ went to Madrid for tropical trials, then Dubai for measured runway take-offs and climb performance in hot climates, both with and without booster assistance. While in Dubai, the air conditioning system was tested.

With its flight-testing duties complete, G-AWZA was handed over to BEA in December for crew training. While on this training programme on 19 January 1971 at RAE Bedford, the aircraft flew too low while practising overshooting and struck the tail of Comet 3B G-ANLO on the runway threshold, removing the fin and rudder. The Comet was removed from the runway, and the Trident made a flapless landing; both aircraft were repaired.

The Trident 3B was awarded its C of A on 8 February 1971 and entered service with BEA on 11 March, when G-AWZC flew from London to Madrid. BEA's Trident 3s served many European destinations, particularly when in November G-AWZK landed at Schiphol from London when all other aircraft were grounded by fog. After six months of passenger operations, BEA expressed total satisfaction with the Trident 3B, departure reliability running at 96 per cent, which was well in advance of the reliability of the Trident 1s and 2s at a similar stage in service. Trident 3s were the most reliable airliner ever to enter service with the airline, with automatic fault identification greatly reducing maintenance delays. With a mixed fleet of sixty-four new Tridents and six second-hand examples, BEA had the benefit of fleet commonality. Trident were finally withdrawn from British Airways (which had been created by a merger with BOAC in 1974) on 31 December 1985, unable to comply with new engine noise regulations.

Chinese Tridents

With the sale of PIA Tridents to CAAC of China, a relationship was created between Hawker Siddeley and the Chinese Legation at Blackheath in London. A Chinese team was invited to Hatfield, where their first impression was that Hatfield must be a car factory as employee cars filled the car parks. They had just come through the Cultural Revolution and their technology was limited. Following this visit, an HSA team from Hatfield visited China in March 1971, and after very intense negotiations, CAAC ordered six in August, followed a year later by another six Trident 2Es with an option on a further six.

These options were taken up three months later, in addition to an order for two extended range Trident Super 3Bs. Soon after, on 19 November 1972, the first Trident was delivered to China by John and the Hatfield team. With a final order for another fifteen Trident 2Es in December 1973, total orders by China amounted to thirty-three aircraft, valued at £120 million at 1973 prices. This kept the Trident production line open from 1973 until 1978, with the 117th and last Trident leaving Hatfield on 28 June 1978. The final delivery was on a repaired Trident 2E that had suffered an in-flight fire during testing. It was delivered by John and Peter Bugge on 13 September 1978.

Although John had flown aircraft all over the world, deliveries to China were a totally new experience. He took Des Penrose as co-pilot on the first delivery, Des being responsible for navigation. John and the technical team were all ready to depart when BEA Trident 1 G-ARPI crashed at Staines after take-off from Heathrow on 18 June 1972, entering a deep stall early on the climb out and killing all on board. John had to stay around for the inquiry, but he found that the pilot, Captain Key, had suffered a heart attack and died as the aircraft climbed away, and an inexperienced junior pilot had retracted the wing leading droop prematurely.

John and his team finally departed from Hatfield on 19 November 1972 after a formal handover at Hatfield on 13 November, when the third CAAC Trident 2E order was announced. The China Tridents were in full CAAC livery, but with UK registrations. Refuelling stops were made at Istanbul, Dubai, and Sri Lanka, from where a departure was made at midnight the following day to arrive at Kwangchow at the correct time. The aircraft was not permitted to overfly India, Cambodia, or Laos for diplomatic reasons. A refuelling stop was made at Kuala Lumpur, although Chinese-marked aircraft were not entirely welcome. The route then took them to Hong Kong, flying in the direction of the Philippines to avoid being intercepted by Chinese Nationalist aircraft over the Formosa Straits. The Trident arrived at Hong Kong at lunchtime, when John had to check the airfield at Kwangchow, where the short 100-mile flight was expected at precisely 4 p.m.

After a very long delivery flight, the crew were exhausted, and had no idea what to expect in the form of a welcome, but they were met by the head of CAAC and his team, who had arranged a reception followed by a formal banquet, which became typical of all future deliveries. A little later, John tactfully suggested that it may be better to hold the celebration on the day after arrival, which was agreed upon without hesitation. The team was accommodated in the transit hotel for two weeks or more. It lacked modern amenities like refrigerators, air conditioning, and food. John and the team worked closely with the Chinese acceptance engineers; if an item was suspect, rather than argue, it would be replaced. The CAAC pilots had all flown in the Peoples' Republic Air Force and were keen to fly Tridents.

All acceptance programmes included an 800-mile test flight with a Chinese crew from Kwangchow to Shanghai, the flight taking place in the morning with John flying. On arrival at Shanghai, there would be a tour of one of the local factories followed by a good lunch. John and the team were able to wander around the rather drab city, lacking in colour and stylish clothes. They would then fly back to Kwangchow at night when the CAAC pilots would take over with John in the right-hand seat. The following day would be spent sorting out queries, followed by the acceptance ceremony and banquet, when John and the CAAC airline director signed the documents. The documents would then go to Peking, and payment made to Hawker Siddeley account in Hong Kong, usually within two weeks. John and the team would take the train to Hong Kong from where they would fly home.

Following his accident in the HS 125 at Dunsfold, John suffered two crushed vertebrae, but he suffered no long-term effects and was able to return to flying in 1976. By then, he was fifty-eight years old and would normally have retired, but when the Chinese heard of his impending retirement, it was made quite clear that they wanted his services to continue and would not accept any substitute. John was therefore able to enjoy three more years of visiting China. He said that the Chinese did not like salesmen but they worked well with engineers and technicians; John himself was a very effective, but unassuming salesman. He retired from what had become British Aerospace in 1980.

Having made the decision to give up flying when he retired, John had many other interests, including his love of the Hertfordshire countryside. He was most hospitable to friends and colleagues when they visited him, and he worked hard in his garden growing and canning his many vegetables, including carrots. John was an enthusiastic trustee of the de Havilland Aircraft Museum, supporting its growth and development—in particular leaving a substantial bequest when he died. Despite losing much of his hard-earned funds as a name with Lloyds of London, he recovered and also left a substantial sum to the Geoffrey de Havilland Flying Foundation, of which he was chairman. Probably the last time John was on the flight deck was on 20 July 1996, when the author took him to Boscombe Down for a flight on Comet 4C XS235 *Canopus* to celebrate as close as possible the forty-ninth anniversary of the maiden flight of the Comet.

Philip Birtles, the author of this biography, was John's PA for seven and a half years during the Trident flight development programme; we became very good friends. On one of many visits to John, I volunteered to cut his substantial area of grass. With difficulty, we both managed to start the sit-on mower, which ran only when there was the weight of a person in the seat. The author said to John that he would not have to worry about cutting his grass again as he would take care of it. John died on 21 July 2002, only two weeks later, just short of his eighty-fifth birthday. His memorial service was at St Nicholas' Church in Harpenden. A memorial to John is located at the de Havilland Aircraft Museum, together with his Harmon Trophy, of which he was very proud; his Caterpillar Club badge, which he received after abandoning the Moth Minor with Geoffrey Jnr; and other memorabilia.

Despite his modest nature and desire for privacy, John Cunningham was honoured in both military and civil aviation. On the military side, in addition to the Second World War campaign medals awarded to those who fought, he received the Distinguished Service Order (DSO) and two Bars and the Distinguished Flying Cross and Bar. Such a tally is quite remarkable. He also received awards from Britain's allies during the conflict—the Silver Star from the United States and the Order of the Patriotic War from the Soviet Union.

On the civil side, he was made a Commander of the British Empire (CBE) and received the Award of Honour from the Guild of Air Pilots and Air Navigators (now the Honourable Company of Air Pilots) for the year 2000–2001. Established in 1929 as a City Guild and Livery Company of London, the guild has actively promoted excellence in British aviation. The award is given to 'an individual who has made an outstanding lifetime contribution to aviation'. Unsurprisingly, Cunningham became involved in other charities and organisations having their roots in British aviation both military and civilian—the RAF Benevolent Fund, the Battle of Britain Fighter Association, the RAF Club in Piccadilly, and the Geoffrey de Havilland Flying Foundation; he was also a trustee of the de Havilland Aircraft Museum, which he supported with great enthusiasm. He was a deputy lieutenant for Middlesex in 1948 and Greater London in 1965.

When Group Captain John Cunningham died on 21 July 2002, he was mourned by many. The penultimate paragraph of the Guild of Air Pilots and Air Navigators 'Award of Honour' describes him succinctly:

> In both peace and war John Cunningham demonstrated inspired
> leadership, infinite patience, and an easy mastery of new techniques
> and challenges. His superb flying skill, coupled with his vision,
> determination, and courage, matched by personal courtesy and
> modesty, have deservedly earned him the esteem of the nation and the
> world-wide respect of his profession.

8

Testing Moments

Sir Geoffrey liked to keep in touch with all DH goings-on. In the factory, he was a familiar figure, sauntering unassertively around shop floors and hangars, nodding to all, apprentices and managers alike. His comprehensive greeting to everyone he knew, or hadn't even seen before, was 'Good morning! How are you getting on?'

To keep in touch with his high-level people, he invited them to his office for shop-talk and Miss Chapman's tea and scones. Top of his call list was chief test pilot John Cunningham. In Sir Geoffrey's experience, flight testing is the affirmation of nearly every department's end-product.

He took no formal notes—a loss to air history—but we know the events which he and JC (as he was sometimes known) would have discussed. In 'Testing Moments', transcribed from tapes for the first time in full, we have the chief test pilot's first-hand evidence of what actually happened. The questions are ours (Mike Ramsden and John Hellings) but we believe they resonate with Geoffrey de Havilland's. JC took our questions with no preview; every answer was on the record and afterwards he deleted nothing.

Sir Geoffrey appointed JC chief test pilot in September 1946 when Geoffrey Jnr, GdeH's son, was killed flying the high-speed DH.108

TG306 experimental jet. In the next thirty-three years (1946–1979), Cunningham was the first to fly thirty new de Havilland types, including the Comet 1, the world's first jet airliner.

He was responsible or answerable for the testing of production as well as experimental aircraft. He was also headmaster of the company's airfields and flight-test staff at Hatfield and other DH test bases.

Aerospace life in those days was busy and innovating, full of ideas and new projects. The de Havilland offices, departments, and bustling factory floors were never short of flight-test news. As the years approached Cunningham's retirement (1979), his friends, colleagues, and staff urged him to talk about his interesting incidents. Among the successful persuaders were John Hellings, John Loader, Mike Ramsden, and John Wilson. Over a pint or two in The Fox (where the landlord had presented Cunningham with his own chair), he consented, begging in his self-effacing way to be spared a full autobiography. Would he agree to an interview with his de Havilland colleagues—people who had worked for him and knew how he and DH ticked? He did not say no.

At his home, he agreed to an interview about the 'testing moments' of his flying career. His legendary RAF service as a night-fighter ace had made an acceptable book, but it covered only 10 per cent of his flying career. The missing 90 per cent—his post-war work as a civilian test pilot—was the big gap that needed to be filled.

At last, twenty years after retiring, JC sat down with a microphone and interviewers. His words would enhance the national aviation archives and benefit the Geoffrey de Havilland Flying Foundation, the de Havilland Aircraft Museum and the Royal Aeronautical Society, all charities supporting the ambitions of future pilots and aerospace engineers. JC served the three charities as chairman, director and fellow respectively.

The *JC Tapes* sold out and are here followed by a text version, *Testing Moments*. Published in the following pages, the conversations include original unpublished tape 'rescued from the cutting room floor'. They also include JC quotes remembered by colleagues.

The tapes needed the customary light editing of unrehearsed and unscripted conversation without affecting sense or meaning. The editing has been limited to smoothing the flow, readability, clarity, and continuity. The square brackets signify technical explanations and the deletion of inaudible and indistinct 'talking-over' passages.

Testing Moments

Q. Thank-you for agreeing to this interview. We would like to start with your 'interesting moment' as a junior DH test pilot in 1938. You had finished your engineering apprenticeship at the DH Tech School and joined Geoffrey de Havilland Jnr's flight-test team. You were checking the first production DH.94 Moth Minor before its certification tests. [The two-seat Moth Minor was the precursor of DH Canada's Chipmunk primary trainer of 1946]. Geoffrey agreed to fly with you in case of clangers. You were in the rear seat and while you were testing the stall and spin-recovery the aeroplane failed to recover, the engine stopped and you both baled out. Wasn't that your first and only bale-out?

A. Yes, just the one. After we had jumped out the aircraft recovered from its spin and the Gipsy engine restarted. I watched the aeroplane flying happily round and round with nobody in it. The real lesson of that incident was our failure to turn off the switches and close the throttles. Beggars belief!

Q. Did Geoffrey order 'Get out'?

A. No, I did that. Geoffrey had said: 'There's no response from my flying controls,' and I had replied: 'There's no response from mine either. We've got to get out.'

Q. This was all discussed through Gosport tubes?

A. Yes—we had no electric intercom.

Q. You both watched the aeroplane flying round and round after baling out?

A. Yes, very much so—not only could we see it. We could hear the thing. It eventually crashed into a big oak tree and destroyed itself.

Q. Where exactly did it come down?

A. Opposite Lamer Lodge in Wheathampstead. That's where I took the photographs. I used to carry a camera in case anything unusual or interesting occurred.

Q. You had no idea where Geoffrey had landed?

A. No idea. I was out well before he was. The Moth Minor came down almost gently. Geoff had said in his preflight safety briefing that he would delay any jump so that he didn't come down on my head. The aeroplane was very close when it came past me. Looking down I thought Geoffrey seemed to be half way out on the wing [when he pulled his rip-cord]. He drifted off out of my view. Taking photographs on the ground I was concerned about him until some people appeared, pointing towards the lower Luton Road.

It was quite clear in my mind that Geoffrey, wherever he had come down, would be in The Crooked Chimney [the DH test pilots' popular pub at Lemsford]. I stopped a passing motorist who kindly gave me a lift and, sure enough, Geoff was in the pub, speaking to Hatfield. Some DH people turned up. The police arrived but seemed unconcerned about aeroplanes falling out of the sky and crashing and burning. There was no excitement at all. We bundled our parachutes into a car and returned to Hatfield.

Q. Was the Moth Minor modified?

A. Yes—bigger fin and rudder areas and travel.

Q. Then came World War 2. You and your radar observer scored 20 victories at night, in the course of which you must have experienced many interesting moments. Although this interview is about your life as a civilian test pilot, you had two memorable Mosquito incidents while wearing military and civil hats simultaneously. What was all that about?

A. In 1941, soon after the prototype Mosquito W4050's first flight, Sir Geoffrey asked RAF chief Lord Portal if he would allow me to assess the Mosquito's suitability as a night-fighter. Portal, the RAF's great leader throughout the war, sent for me: 'You are probably wondering why I wanted to see you. Your former boss, Sir Geoffrey de Havilland, has asked me if you would evaluate his new

Mosquito as a night fighter ... Off I went in my Beaufighter from Middle Wallop to Hatfield.

Geoffrey Jnr, chief test pilot at Hatfield during the war, briefed me. I sat in the single pilot's seat and had a good look round at things. I remember Geoff saying that the elevator trim was 'approximately down there, on your left. You'll find it easily when you're in the air'. He couldn't fly with me because the prototype was a single-pilot aeroplane [and still is—W4050 is preserved by the DH Museum at St Albans]. I wasn't sure about all the fuel cocks and I suggested that a Hatfield flight engineer would be welcome. A very good chap called Tony Arthur came with me. He had a wooden leg, I recall.

The Mosquito's throttles were dreadful, piddling things with little movement between a Merlin idling and a Merlin at full power. The undercarriage selector [UP/DOWN] belonged to one of the Airspeed Consuls being built at Hatfield.

We got started and taxied out—Hatfield was a grass airfield in those days. I went off in the St Albans direction, heading 24. As soon as I got off the ground, with one hand on the throttles and the other on the flying controls, I had to get the wheels up. Having tightened up the throttle friction nut as hard as possible I was about to select wheels up when one of the throttles moved back of its own accord, reducing the power of that engine [and inducing a strong asymmetric situation]. The aeroplane wasn't in trim and I couldn't find the tail trimmer: you had to feel for it down on the left—I remembered Geoffrey saying 'trim is approximately down there'. Well, I could have got the aeroplane in trim but I couldn't take my hand off the controls to select wheels up. So I jammed my knees round the flying controls, long enough for me to tighten the throttles and select wheels up. The people on the airfield must have wondered what in hell was going on up there. When we got back and Geoff asked if we'd enjoyed ourselves I said: 'Yes, thank you, very much, but your throttle friction nut is ...' 'Oh,' he said, 'sorry, I meant to tell you about that.'

Q. When you had sorted these things out did you put the aircraft through its paces and recommend that the Mosquito would make a good night-fighter?

A. I flew it just as I would fly a new aircraft type. The Mosquito was a lovely flying aeroplane, 100 m.p.h. faster than the Beaufighter. I said that a Mosquito NF would without a shadow of a doubt be a marvellous development—ideal for the job, with the radar picture [of the target] in sight of the pilot and the observer alongside him. It was clear that the Mosquito's internal layout would allow the radar picture and observer to be up forward. In the Beaufighter they were down the back behind the pilot. The first Mosquito night-fighter squadron was formed in late 1941 but I didn't get one until the end of 1943.

Q. Rather a long wait?

A. Yes but the Beaufighter was a fine machine and it did its work very well.

Q. When you eventually got Mosquitos didn't you have another spot of bother with the throttles?

A. Yes. In 1943 the Mosquito XV was conjured up quickly with radar and increased wingspan to deal with the 45,000-ft German [Ju86Ps] which were coming over taking photos and dropping bombs. To improve the Mosquito's maximum ceiling everything on board was lightened. When you took off you could see the extended wing-tips bending up. The cannon were taken out, leaving us with only our machine-guns in the nose. And, oh dear, the throttle levers were lightened.

The Mosquito's throttles were pretty dreadful anyway. We received two Mk XVs at RAF Hunsdon. That night the pair of us were to go to 45,000ft to check that the radar worked. Well, if you can believe this, when I moved the two throttle levers to full power one of them came off in my hand. Lovely. I was now off the ground at full power with one throttle lever. The other had broken at its root. Now what? Do I carry on and fiddle with things? Do I try to put my fingers in to see if I can pull the throttle back? Marvellous! A special lightweight throttle. Once again, Hatfield's desire for lightness. At least I was in the air and I could probably turn engine switches on and off.

Q. What did you decide to do?

A. Carry on and stay with the other Mosquito, already in the air with me. We wanted to make sure that our radars worked properly at over 45,000ft. The new AI radar was a great departure for the Mosquito. It was very successful, with a clear radar picture, and the radar observer was alongside the pilot instead of down the back, as in the Beaufighter.

Q. It's said that you were, and still are, the only RAF pilot to have evaluated a new military aircraft before Boscombe Down pilots got their hands on it.

A. Yes, I think that's right.

Q. Your most challenging experimental work, would you agree, came after the war with the DH.108 jet, a scaled down DH.106 jet airliner, then still a project. [In 1946 the high speed DH.108, TG 306, broke up at 'a speed greater than previously attained by man', killing Geoffrey de Havilland Jnr., Sir Geoffrey's son and chief test pilot.]. Two more DH.108s were built: the low-speed TG 283 and the supersonic VW120. In these aircraft you made more than 150 flights, many to extreme limits, to find the cause of GdeH Jnr's death. During your investigation didn't you do many stalls with DH.108 TG 283 and high-Mach dives with VW120?

A. Yes, and I found when testing TG 283's stall recovery that instead of the aircraft 'falling', only a wing was doing this, and only slightly. The nose wasn't falling as it should so I had   to push the stick forward. Instead of recovering the aircraft fell over sideways and forwards. I found myself on my back and in a spin.

Q. An uncontrolled spin upside down, with the ground fast approaching and rotating 'above' you? At what sort of height were you, and how did you recover?

A. Somewhere around 7,000 ft or 8,000 ft I think. I was taken totally by surprise. I'd never been in an aeroplane which went over sideways instead of going down and over or rolling over. Looking out of the cockpit I had no doubt that sideways was the way I was going. I had never known an aeroplane do that. It then went into its upside-down spin. I pressed the button or pulled the lever or whatever to get the spin chutes out [small parachutes fitted to the wingtips of the DH.108 to help recovery from an uncontrollable spin]. To my horror almost as soon as the drag chutes came out the aircraft wing-tip vortices just spun the chutes round and round. I saw them both closing right up, useless. They didn't do anything. I thought, well, it's up to me now, there's nothing more I can do except fiddle with full rudder, the only effective control I had. I was able to slow the spin down until it stopped. Still upside down, I got my flaps and wheels fully out and recovered in the last half of what would have been a loop.

By then I was at 3,000ft or 4,000ft, and not far from Hatfield. Oh dear, what a performance! As soon as I got back to my office I rang the Royal Aircraft Establishment and said: 'Your anti-spin chutes don't work—they wind themselves up almost immediately in the tip vortices.' They replied: 'Ooh, we'll follow this up'. What had happened was that our design people, and those at the RAE Farnborough, had failed to realise that if you put a spin chute on something, it must have a swivelling attachment [or it won't inflate]. I thought oh well, so much for the Royal Aircraft Establishment's anti-spin chutes. The RAE or our design people, I'm not sure who, hadn't realised ... well, we won't go into that!

Q. Which 108 were you flying?

A. The low-speed one, TG 283. When Geoffrey was killed in the first 108, the high-speed TG 306, TG 283 had permanently fixed open slats. That was the 108 which I inherited from Geoffrey. I did more than a year's flight-testing in it to learn everything we could from Geoffrey's accident and from the 108's layout [highly swept-wings with elevons; a fin and rudder but no tail plane]. Then came the high-speed DH.108 VW120, the first Hatfield aeroplane with an ejection seat.

Q. Wasn't there an ejection seat in TG 283?

A. No, I just sat on my parachute. That DH.108 survived our eighteen months of low-speed work, right up to when [having briefed RAE Farnborough] we handed it over to them. Sadly, it caught them out too.

Q. They lost the aircraft and a test pilot in May 1950, didn't they?

A. Sqn/Ldr G.E.C. Genders. The same thing happened to him, maybe not exactly the same but, well, he would have wanted to try things out for himself. He eventually decided to jump. TG283 still had no ejection seat. He was either too late getting out or he hit the fin. The aircraft came down near Farnborough.

Q. Can you tell us about the DH.108 incident causing you to abort a take-off at Hatfield?

A. That was also TG283 [before it went to Farnborough]. The concrete runway at Hatfield was 6,000ft plus grass overruns. I had lifted off about a third of the way along the runway when I sensed that the stick didn't feel right—something had gone astray. I decided to put the thing back on the runway. The 108's deceleration was marvellous and I didn't need to pull the wheels up to stop. Its thin wheels and high-pressure tyres ran off the end of the concrete into soft earth. And there I was, stuck in the mud [near St Albans Road and Notcutts garden centre].

Q. Your take-off checks hadn't indicated anything amiss with the controls?

A. Nothing, but in the air I didn't get the response which I should have done so I put it back on the runway.

Q. Did you walk back to your office or what?

A. A towing vehicle of some kind appeared and the aircraft was moved smoothly and undamaged onto concrete.

Q. What was found to be the cause of that incident?

A. The DH.108's powered flying controls had no centring and the friction had been adjusted in a way which made me feel something was wrong as soon as I got into the air. It was put right and it never happened again.

Q. On the high-speed DH.108 side of things: how did you investigate exactly what Geoffrey had been doing when he was killed?

A. One did this in extremely small steps of increasing speed. I was well aware that DH.108 VW120 had the most efficient and clean wing we had ever flown, and that its de Havilland Goblin engine, a relatively low-powered turbojet, was able to achieve about

Mach .88 level at 35,000ft—level, not diving. That was an amazing performance at the time. Even today, 50 years later, not many things are cruising at 0.88 on 3,000lb of thrust.

But pitch-damping of the tailless DH.108, especially in turbulence, was dreadful – almost nil. Geoff's problem was high Mach low down in turbulence [a combination of high drag and low pitch control]. The whole thing up-ended and the wings came off, downwards. As far as I was concerned a large tailless airliner would be hopeless [at that time the DH.106 jetliner project on Sir Geoffrey's drawing-board looked much like the DH.108].

Q. When did you first advise that the Comet jet airliner must have a tailplane?

A. Oh, immediately after flying the first 108 [laughter]. As far as I was concerned Bishop and Clarkson [chief designer and chief aerodynamicist] hadn't a hope in heaven of Comet pitch control without tailplane. And there was much to learn from the DH.108's swept-wing. The DH.110 fighter was nothing other than a 108 with a large tail. [The Trident's wings were the fastest in airline service—see below—and the wings of every Airbus have been designed and built in Britain [all with the genes of the DH.108's wing].

Q. How many DH.108 flights did you do investigating Geoffrey Jnr's death?

A. We'll have to look in my logbook for that [about 150]. At that time it was almost entirely '108 high Mach'. We needed to find the point at which pitch-stability in turbulence became negative. In turbulence you could see and feel it immediately you pulled up the wheels. It would have been ludicrously hazardous to go much beyond the point where Geoffrey was killed [at low altitude].

Q. Was that why you went up high to do high-speed testing?

A. Yes, we did the ['sound-barrier'] work from 35,000ft. John Derry joined us from Supermarine and he started from up high.

Q. In your investigation of Geoffrey's death did you go to the same Mach number at which he was killed?

A. Yes, probably, but not at the same IAS [indicated air speed at high-altitudes].

Q. Were you troubled by much turbulence?

A. Yes.

Q. Can you say you enjoyed this sort of flying, or was it tempered with a sort of …?

A. Well of course I was determined to find out all we could about the cause of Geoffrey's death —what had actually gone on. After that accident most of my 108 flying—for nearly a year until the high-speed DH.108 VW120 came along—was in the slow-speed TG283. I remember doing the first flights of VW120 and the Ghost Lanc. on the same day in July 1947 [the outboard Merlins of the Lancaster were replaced by Ghost jets to be tested for de Havilland's airliner project].

Q. Those were innovative days. Wasn't that the first air test of the Ghost jet engine for the Comet?

A. Yes, and all to good purpose. You asked how many DH.108 VW120 high-speed flights we did. They went on from 10 August, alternating between VW120 at Mach .83, more TG283 stalls, further jet Lancaster tests for DH Engines, and so on. All in a day's work!

Q. Full envelope indeed. Did Derry and Wilson share 108 work?

A. Yes. I see that at the end of August we were practising for Derry's 108 attempt on the 100km close-circuit world speed record.

Q. A sign of confidence in the stability and control of the 108?

A. Yes, entirely.

Q. Derry broke the world speed record, didn't he? Wasn't there some concern about turbulence and you wanted to check this before Derry's attempt?

A. I went round the course in a Vampire and was happy that conditions would be perfectly all right for John. He did it in 108 VW120, not the same circuit but the same 100 km distance in the Hatfield area. He got a much higher speed than my 496 mph—600 mph plus, I think.

Q. John Derry later touched Mach 1 indicated in VW120 didn't he?

A. Yes, he did.

Q. Is it correct to say that, flying the DH.108, an aircraft with normal jet power and normal take-off and landing, Derry was the world's first normally equipped pilot to go supersonic?

A. Yes, I think that's true. [The American Bell X-1 had rockets, not a jet engine; it had to be lifted off the ground by a B-29 bomber up to high altitude. Bell's Slick Goodlin and later the US Air Force's Chuck Yeager went supersonic in the X-1 but they had rocket not jet power and had to land as gliders.

Q. As Derry's boss you knew what he was doing?

A. Yes, entirely. We both had the Aerodynamics Department's test programme. I didn't control what John Derry wanted to do, or the way he wanted to do it.

Q. Were you surprised when he touched Mach 1 in the 108, or was that planned and discussed?

A. It was part of the programme. One was grateful that nothing disastrous happened, thank God. It wasn't very clever from the control point of view—Derry had problems recovering from a [bunt] in one dive [see pages 191-194]. But that was a feature of the aeroplane and, yes, it was not surprising.

Q. Did Derry get a pat on the back for that?

A. Oh yes. John was a fine person and a very fine pilot.

Q. He was thought of as a good showman, wasn't he?

A. He was a brilliant demonstration pilot. That's how I first became aware of him, when he was with Supermarine. I used to see the air displays and quickly realised that he was a person who knew exactly what he was doing. Supermarine was giving him dull aeroplanes to test, the Swift for one. They were not very successful—the company seemed to decline after the Spitfire. I thought I would speak to the chief test pilot, Jeffrey Quill, whom I knew well, and say that I would like to ask John Derry if he would join us at Hatfield. We had plenty of 108 development work and my hands were full. Jeffrey said, 'I would be delighted to let him go because you'll make good use of him.'

Q. Do you recall the new control tower and offices overlooking Hatfield airfield? One day you looked out of a window saying 'I remember this exact bit of sky. I was trying to land a DH.110 Sea Vixen across the runway instead of along it'. Why would you have been trying to do that?

A. Bish wanted us to check that the flexibility of the 110's twin booms wouldn't jam the flying controls. For the test the rudders were locked or limited. When landing I couldn't get the aeroplane to line up with the runway and I had to go around and land across it on to the grass.

Q. Not perhaps the best Sea Vixen deck-landing approach procedure?

A. The stretched Comets too were also flexible in turbulence. I noticed a strange resonance in the cockpit of the long-fuselage Comet 3. Bish agreed that it was unacceptable and I suggested that we should compare it with the long-fuselage Lockheed Super Constellation, and in turbulence. We approached friends in KLM who kindly arranged all I wanted to do. I had to tell Bish that I was sorry, but … So he specified thicker fuselage skin which solved the problem. The 110's twin booms were also made thicker and stiffer.

Q. Could you tell us about your DH.110 Sea Vixen's electrical power failure over Heathrow in 1951?

A. Oh dear—the 110's electrical power system. The aircraft had Rolls-Royce Avon engines and each one had a generator-failure warning-light in front of me. We were in the early stages of flying the 110—I had flown it only three or four times since the first flight in 1951 – and we were preparing to measure performance at height. I used to start over Germany – there were no restrictions as to where you went in those 20,000ft propeller days. We flew at about 35,000ft from overhead Lakenheath to Boscombe. Both had long runways so I always went between them in case we had to go down for any reason.

I was nearing Boscombe at about 35,000ft when a red light came on. Generator failure, oh dear. I was set to turn towards Lakenheath to continue temperature calibration at 35,000ft, instrumentation checks and so on. The 110 was cleverly all-electric. Well, I was never keen on all that – fuel pumps in the wings to fill the small gravity tank behind the cockpit and another electric pump in that tank to feed the engines.

Half-way from Boscombe towards Lakenheath I got a second red light. To save weight this clever new electrical system limited the capacity of the batteries to sustain electrical demand for about two minutes—or less. I couldn't speak to Tony Richards, my observer down on the right-hand side. Then everything electrical failed: all my engine instruments, flight instruments, even my intercom so that I couldn't talk to Tony.

I looked out of the cockpit and saw a small hole in a cloud through which I recognised a Heathrow runway. That fixed me—I knew where I was. Realising that I would be speechless in a few moments I called Hatfield and got as far as saying: 'Tell London ...' when my message was cut off.

The tail trim, also electrical, had to counter the enormous trim-change which landing flaps introduced. And the wing tanks were below the engines on the 110 so they needed more electric pumps. I decided to keep the engines idling. I wasn't going to do anything more than that. I made my descent from 35,000 feet flapless for a flapless landing at London. I couldn't trim the tail with full flaps anyway. I was clean.

Q. The flaps were hydraulic weren't they?

A. Yes. as were the flying controls, all hydraulic. As long as I could keep the engines rotating ...

Q. Did you have a ram-air turbine?

A. Not on DH.110 WG236 [the prototype]. Such niceties came later. Anyway, I didn't dive or go rushing down. I just hoped to position myself so that when we broke cloud I would be in the circuit or vicinity of Heathrow with time to look around and see what was on the ground or coming into land. I had made up my mind that even if there were things on the runway I was going to land alongside them, because Heathrow's runways are wide enough.

Q. You couldn't have done a go-around?

A. No, no—not at all, and I was anxious to get on the ground before the electric fuel-pumps stopped, when I would have lost control. We weren't going to lose the aeroplane or jump out or anything like that. When we broke cloud we found reasonable visibility beneath and I decided to land on runway 28L, which was vacant. Wheels down and locked, I recall some Hunting maintenance hangars on our left. I made a good flapless landing onto the runway, turned off onto the grass and stopped. Tony was all right [trying, it was reported, not to laugh]. We did the main checks and climbed out. A fire engine arrived. I said to the fireman: 'So sorry about this but all's well, the aircraft is clear of the runway and it isn't blocking anything. Please carry on.' The emergency services recovered the aircraft to Hunting's area. And that was the end of tiny weight-saving electric batteries powering everything, above all the tail-trim control—an absolute failure as far as I was concerned. It led to hydraulic tail-trim and the end of the DH.110's all-electric systems.

Q. Was there any conflicting traffic?

A. I remember there was a Viking taxying towards the runway. It wasn't upsetting me. Nothing else. I also remember the surprising silence [of electrical failure]. No radio voices, no air traffic calls.

Q. You hadn't overtaken anybody on the approach?

A. No, I wasn't wasting a candle on that anyway.

Q. Did they offer you coffee or tea?

A. I offered them my apologies: 'Very sorry about this, I had a total electrical failure'.

Q. And that happened when you were at 35,000ft above cloud with no instruments?

A. I had only a [mechanical standby] airspeed indicator and altimeter. We were descending in clear air when I saw the hole in the cloud and recognised the Heathrow runway.

Q. That was very smart airport recognition, wasn't it?

A. Well one got used to that. You see, most of my flying had been at around 35,000ft—endless flights and heights. One knew the ground at a glance and often recognised a particular item which told you where you were. In this case Heathrow.

Q. Flight-testing the Comet, the world's first jetliner, must have been a huge job. You and your flight-test team got certificates of airworthiness for more than half a dozen versions with few incidents. We know that airline service resulted in the disastrous Comet 1 structural fatigue failures, but did your part of the Comet 1 flight-test programme go as smoothly as it seemed to do? Were the rumours of flutter exaggerated? Wasn't there quite a serious Comet prototype incident when you were trying to provoke flutter? [sudden heavy vibration at speed threatening structural failure].

A. Flutter, yes, and we lost the starboard elevator mass balance. During the previous one or two flights in the prototype Comet 'VG we had what I called a touch of flutter. It was coming from the rudder or elevator, I wasn't sure which—the tail anyway. We spent about an hour and a half one Sunday morning flying 'VG trying to find and record this flutter.

Q. Did you often do your test-flying at weekends?

A. Yes, hangar work on test aircraft was done on weekdays, so weekends were 'all yours'. On this occasion I had booked the Comet Hotel in Hatfield for the flight-crew's lunch. I think I had just said 'we still haven't found the flutter and it's nearly one o'clock'. So I lowered the nose and I think reduced power slightly. Down we went for lunch. Hardly had we started to descend when the flutter began, took charge and built up in a big way. I thought the aircraft was going to fall apart and if I didn't do something it would break up. I pulled back all engine power and applied the airbrakes.

Q. Did you have parachutes?

A. No [the programme was past that stage]. The aerodynamics department's flutter expert John Wimpenny was with us and we'd been flying level for an hour and a half trying to repeat the condition. [When we got it] my concern was to slow the aircraft down and get out of what I'd got into. The flutter was enormous, but it began to die down. We were under control again and landed. We saw that a starboard elevator's underside external mass balance weight had departed, tearing off some elevator skin with it. Clearly a case of elevator flutter. I reckon we had escaped total disaster by just a few moments. There was a design rethink about mass balances and rod-operated flying controls.

Q. Hydraulic screwjacks?

A. That's right.

Q. Was that the worst Comet flutter you experienced?

A. I'm sure it was.

Q. More important, did you get to lunch on time?

A. Yes, but that was a close-run thing too!

Q. Did flutter specialist John Wimpenny's job include flight crew duties?

A. No, but Wimpenny and all the technical staff were keenly interested to see, hear and feel in-flight problems for themselves.

Q. What was the problem when a Comet's flying controls jammed in flight? Do you remember that?

A. Yes, vaguely.

Q. The Air Registration Board chief pilot, David Davies, was pushing and pulling g when a loose shot-bag flew into an open floor-hatch and jammed the 'sheaving-unit' cables of the flying-controls.

A. That's right, I remember now.

Q. Nobody observed this startling event but Tony Fairbrother sensed that something was wrong and Brackstone-Brown helped him to extricate the very heavy shot-bag.

A. One survives these things.

Q. Other Comet 1 anxious moments were your Comet 1A tail-scraping take-offs at Hatfield, following a Canadian Pacific crash at Karachi killing the delivery crew and the DH service engineers. This followed a similar but non-fatal BOAC Comet 1 take-off crash at Rome. Can you tell us what went wrong?

A. After the BOAC take-off incident we reviewed take-off speeds, weights, flight-control 'feel', wing aerodynamics, cockpit illumination at night, crew-training and so on. BOAC Comet pilots had made hundreds of take-offs without incident. I flew the chief pilot of Canadian Pacific in the new Comet 1A, which he was soon to deliver. He sat in the left seat, I sat in the right. Down the Hatfield runway we went, grinding the make-shift keel-strake, tail down, nose in the air. When I'd demonstrated how far back the BOAC stick would have been pulled, and he had experienced runway-scraping tail and sky-scraping nose, he said: 'Holy asterisks, how could he do that? I can't believe it!' A fortnight later at Karachi he and his delivery crew died when he made the same mistake.

Q. That was when you began all those spectacular tail-scraping take-offs at Hatfield. What did you conclude?

A. Propeller-slipstream lift is not produced by jet airliners. A pilot accustomed to propeller airliners might get away with pulling the stick back prematurely, but you can't do that in a jet airliner.

Q. What changes were made to prevent another Comet 1 take-off mistake?

A. Bish 'drooped' the wing's leading edge to improve low-speed lift. There was also stricter calculation and observance of take-off speeds, procedures, manuals and checks.

Q. How did you get along with the DH Trident trijet, the ambitious and very fast short-haul jet airliner of 1962 with a T-tail, three rear mounted Rolls-Royce Speys, and the first 100 per cent blind-landing system?

A. It was a very fine flying machine. The pilots who flew it seemed to be well struck that it was a pretty impressive aeroplane, but it suffered from too little power. That was BEA's idea and its requirement [British European Airways was a regional short-haul airline].

Q. In October 1963 British Aircraft Corporation lost a T-tail rear-engined BAC One-Eleven and all its occupants when it failed to recover from a deep stall. Then in June 1966 Hatfield lost a test Trident and its crew of four in a deep stall. In the following months you performed many hundreds of Trident stalls in search of a safe stall-recovery procedure. Did the aircraft have an automatic stick pusher?

A. Yes, but not right from the start. I flew a Trident with several dozen different stick pushers. Our development flying involved endless stalling, probably mostly without a stick pusher. We had to satisfy ourselves that we could have control without one—which we couldn't. Peter Bugge and I made endless approaches to the stall to establish where one felt the aircraft about to pitch up, the point where an automatic nose-down stick-pusher was essential.

Q. Is a deep stall the point at which the high angle of attack invalidates the elevators?

A. I would say that 'in the stalls' is an extremely difficult place for test flying, knowing that you are right on the edge of an unacceptable condition.

Q. Would it be right to say that the aerodynamics of the Trident's high T-tail, plus the weight of three engines at the back, played their part in causing the deep stall?

A. Oh yes.

Q. It has been said that you did thousands of stalls while developing the Trident, DH.108, Comet and other aircraft. You must have acquired quite a feel for oncoming stalls?

A. Yes, I'm sure you're right.

Q. You really mean thousands?

A. Yes, I am sure of it. This is [a matter of getting a feel] for the oncoming pitch-up. The aeroplane is responding to me when I'm nearest to the pitch-up. When you meet it, that actual moment, you push the stick forward just as quickly as you can.

Q. Presumably sometimes you pushed the stick fully forward, but wouldn't the aircraft just hang there?

A. No, no, I never hung there. No—that would have been the end.

Q. The thing would eventually fall, but wouldn't it take its time?

A. Yes but the aeroplane is counting before you are aware of the pitch-up.

Q. The Trident was very fast, wasn't it, almost too fast for short-hauls?

A. Yes, it missed out. It was useless to BEA [for short hauls] because it had to allow for the slower jets—Caravelles and whatever—in congested air traffic. Just to be the fastest in Europe, which was what BEA claimed, was sad. But the Trident had a very good speed performance.

Q. You had no problems testing that?

A. No, not really. Tony Fairbrother will tell you that we took the Trident up to Mach 0.9 and then up to Mach 0.96, something like that. I thought that the Mach 1 indicated which we had in the

Trident was doubtless due to position error [incorrectly positioned sensor].

Q. Did you get any flutter in the Trident?

A. No, we didn't, although the Trident had quite a big body to force through the air.

Q. Your expertise was to make the right decisions in fast moving 'interesting moments'. The fact that you are sitting here in your armchair suggests that you must have made the right decisions. Were there others which, with hindsight, you would have made differently.

A. Trade secret sir!

Appendix I

Deep-Stall Postscript

After the fatal Trident deep-stall crash in 1966, which killed four of Cunningham's flight-test team, he re-examined the lethal sequence. In one of many stalls the pitch-up seemed to come too soon and he went too deep. Out of control and descending rapidly, he orchestrated engine thrust, flaps, slats, air brakes, even the undercarriage, and 'broke the lock'. The first pilot to slay the T-tail dragon selected the heading for home, sat back and said to his crew: 'I think that's enough for today'.

Appendix II

Sir Geoffrey's Chief Test Pilot

After Whitgift School John Cunningham became an apprentice engineer at the de Havilland Aeronautical Technical School, Hatfield. He learnt to fly with the RAF, and his first job (1937) was with de Havilland as a junior test pilot. In World War 2, 1939–1945, he excelled as an RAF night-fighter pilot, becoming a national celebrity. He and his navigator Sgt Jim Rawnsley shot down 20 enemy bombers using secret British airborne interception radar.

The press called Cunningham 'Cat's Eyes', attributing his night vision to carrots. He never minded the nickname and was delighted when, at his retirement party in 1979, colleagues presented him with a pair of 'Cat's Eyes' road reflectors.

After the war JC rejoined de Havilland as a test pilot. His qualifications as an aircraft engineer were especially helpful at briefings and debriefings with designers, engineers and technical staff.

Sir Geoffrey made him chief test pilot in 1946 when Geoffrey de Havilland Jnr was killed flying the experimental DH.108. For the next thirty years he was responsible for testing more than thirty different types of new de Havilland civil and military aircraft including DH.98 Mosquito variants; DH.100/112/113/115 Vampire and Venom jet fighters; Sea Vampire and Sea Venom carrier jet fighters; DH.103 Hornet Sea Hornet, world's fastest propeller fighter; DH.104 Dove mini airliner; DH.106 Comet, world's first jet airliner (seven Comet Marks) plus three types of Nimrod maritime patrol (Comet derivative) aircraft; DH.108, high-subsonic swept-wing tailless research jet; DH.110 Sea Vixen, first naval twin-jet carrier-based radar fighter-bomber; DH.114 Heron light airliner; DH.121 Trident (three Marks), world's fastest airliner and the first with 100% blind-landing ability; and DH.125, Europe's first business jet.

This de Havilland output of more than thirty new aircraft types was accomplished in thirty years, a feat of engineering innovation described by assistant chief engineer Richard Clarkson as 'unsurpassed by any company in history'. Cunningham and his team were responsible for testing them all.

JC was at the same time responsible for testing aircraft which, though not DH-designed, were fitted with DH equipment—engines, propellers, guided missiles, rockets etc. These aircraft, operated from an independent base at Hatfield, and included an Avro Lancastrian heavy bomber re-engined with two DH Ghost jets for the Comet jetliner; English Electric Lightning Mach 2 jet fighters with DH missiles; a Gloster Javelin jet fighter with DH engines; a Short Sperrin bomber with two DH Gyron jets in place of two of its four Rolls-Royce Avons; an English Electric Canberra fitted with DH Sprite rockets; an Airspeed Ambassador airliner with DH propellers; an Airspeed Horsa commando glider fitted with a Comet nose to test the pilot's view; a DH Canada Chipmunk; a DH Canada DHC-2 Beaver 2; and DH-equipped aircraft.

JC took charge personally of all major new projects—DH.108 experimental jets, DH.106 Comet Mk1-4 jetliners and DH.121 Trident Mk 1–3 jetliners. He assessed many other new types, assigning the project pilots, flight engineers and flight-test staff.

He led the management of the company's airfields: air traffic control, navigation, instrument landing systems and flight-test facilities at Hatfield, Chester, Christchurch and elsewhere. His heaviest ground duty was the constant briefing and debriefing required by the company's design and engineering staff, especially those responsible for performance, stability and control.

JC's two-litre Riley could be observed regularly after hours outside his flight-test office. Born in 1920 he died in 2002 peacefully in his sleep at St Andrew's care home near Hatfield.

Mike Ramsden

Appendix III

German Aircraft Destroyed
/Probably Destroyed/
Damaged by John Cunningham (1940–1944)

With Jimmy Rawnsley on 604 Squadron flying Bristol
Beaufighters

19.11.40	Ju 88	Destroyed at night
23.12.40	He 111	Destroyed at night
02.01.41	He 111	Probable at night
12.01.41	He 111	Damaged at night
15.02.41	He 111	Destroyed at night
12.03.41	He 111	Damaged at night
12.03.41	Ju 88	Damaged at night
03.04.41	He 111	Destroyed at night
07.04.41	He 111	Destroyed at night
09.04.41	He 111	Damaged at night
09.04.41	He 111	Destroyed at night
11.04.41	He 111	Destroyed at night
11.04.41	He 111	Probable at night
15.04.41	He 111	Destroyed at night
15.04.41	He 111	Destroyed at night
15.04.41	He 111	Destroyed at night
03.05.41	He 111	Destroyed at night

07.05.41	He 111	Destroyed at night
01.06.41	He 111	Destroyed at night
22.08.41	He 111	Destroyed at night
22.08.41	He 111	Damaged at night
01.09.41	Ju 88	Destroyed at night
04.04.42	He 111	Damaged in daylight
23.05.42	He 111	Destroyed at night

With Jimmy Rawnsley on 85 Squadron flying de Havilland Mosquitos

13.06.43	Fw 190	Destroyed at night
23.08.43	Fw 190	Destroyed at night
08.09.43	Fw 190	Destroyed at night
02.01.44	Me 410	Destroyed at night
20.02.44	Ju 188	Damaged at night
23.02.44	Ju 188	Probable at night

Aircraft destroyed	20	14 He 111s, 2 Ju 88s, 3 Fw 190s, 1 Me 410
Aircraft probably destroyed	3	2 He 111s, 1 Ju 188
Aircraft damaged	6	4 He 111s, 1 Ju 88, 1 Ju 188